JOSEPH

Living a Life of Integrity

BACK TO THE BIBLE®
Publishing

JOSEPH: Living a Life of Integrity

All Scripture quotations, unless otherwise noted, are taken from the
HOLY BIBLE: NEW INTERNATIONAL VERSION®, copyright © 1973, 1978, 1984 by International Bible Society.
Used by permission of Zondervan Publishing House.
All rights reserved.

All underlining and italicizing of words and phrases in Scripture quotations are added by the authors for
emphasis and clarification.

BACK TO THE BIBLE PUBLISHING
P.O. Box 82808
Lincoln, NE 68501

Editors: Rachel Derowitsch, Allen Bean
Cover and interior design: Robert Greuter & Associates
Art and editorial direction: Kim Johnson

For information about language translations, international availability, and licensing for non-English publication, contact Back to the Bible Publishing at the above address.

Additional copies of this book are available from Back to the Bible Publishing. You may order by calling
1-800-759-2425 or through our Web site at www.resources.backtothebible.org.

1 2 3 4 5 6 7 8 9 10 – 05 04 03 02 01 00

ISBN 0-8474-0202-9

Printed in the USA

CONTENTS

Welcome to our Bible study time together!

Meet Your Bible Study Leaders

Dr. Gene A. Getz is a pastor, church planter, seminary professor, and author of nearly 50 books, including *The Measure of a Man* and the popular *Men of Character* series. Presently, Gene serves as senior pastor at Fellowship Bible Church North in Plano, Texas, and is director of the Center for Church Renewal. He is also host of the syndicated radio program *Renewal*.

Dr. Tony Beckett is the Associate Bible Teacher for the international ministry Back to the Bible. He has pastored churches in Iowa, Ohio, and Pennsylvania, worked with camp ministries and church leadership councils, and served as an area representative for Baseball Chapel. Dr. Beckett and his wife, Joan, have three daughters.

This study on the life of Joseph is another in the *Interacting with God* series. It is our hope and prayer that this approach to Bible study will help you apply God's Word to your daily life.

The *Interacting with God* study guide is intended to do more than teach you basic facts. You still need to know, however, what the Bible says. In order to help with that learning process, each lesson is centered on an event from the life of Joseph. You will learn names, places, and events, all of which are Bible facts that you should know.

Beyond learning what the Bible says, however, you also need to learn what it means for your life today. Woven throughout each lesson are questions to help you do that. These are "interactive" questions written to help you interact with God.

Interacting with God is essentially thinking through what a Scripture passage means for you today. You listen to or read the text, learn what it says, and then think through how to incorporate its truths in your life every day. If you are working through this guide with a group, you will not only think through but also talk through the meaning of each lesson. The Introduction to Interacting with God will help you understand how to best use this study guide.

In Deuteronomy 31:12 Moses instructed the people to "listen and learn to fear the LORD . . . and follow carefully all the words of [the] law." The sequence in this verse is vital! *Listen.* We must first of all be hearers of God's Word. *Learn.* We must do more than just read or hear the words of Scripture. The lessons it contains must be stored in our memory. *Live.* We must put to use (follow) in our daily lives what we learn.

Listen, learn, and live are all vital elements, but they must be kept in that sequence. Application comes after learning. Learning is the result of listening. Start with listening to what the Bible says, learn its truths, and apply them to your life today.

It is our prayer that this Bible study tool will help you explore the Scriptures and respond to God as you develop your personal relationship with Him. We pray that you will experience God's best as you grow more intimate with Him and discover the joy of being a part of a healthy Body of Christ—your church.

Gene A. Getz

Tony Beckett

Introduction to Interacting with God

Even if you have already studied another *Interacting with God* Bible study workbook, you may want to review the following material. These pages are intended to help you get the most out of your study.

Personal and Small-Group Bible Study

This workbook is one course in a series of Bible study tools developed to help Christians experience a dynamic relationship with God. New courses in this series will be released regularly to help you accomplish two primary goals:

1. To know and understand what God is saying to you in the Bible text studied, bringing you to a deeper, more intimate love relationship with Him.

2. Together with other Christians, to grow in your love for one another and increasingly become a healthy and mature Body of Christ that brings glory to God.

Those goals may sound too high or unattainable to you. Indeed, we're not able to accomplish them in our human abilities. Only God can lead His people in such a way that these two goals can be accomplished in your life and in your church. That's why we will be pointing you through the Bible to the Lord and your relationship with Him. As you interact with Him and His Word, the Holy Spirit will guide you and your group to experience God's best. The coming weeks will be a spiritual adventure as God opens your mind to understand and apply His Word to your life, your family, your church, your community, and your world.

If you're not a Christian, don't stop now. We want to help you come to know more about God, so stay with us. This study will help you understand the kind of love relationship God desires to have with you. We will occasionally ask you to examine your relationship with God, knowing that He will be working in your life to reveal Himself and draw you to His Son, Jesus Christ. Being in a small group with other Christians will give you a chance to see up close the difference God makes in a life.

This *Interacting with God* course can be used as either a personal or group Bible study guide. In this introduction we've included suggestions for using this study, but the material is flexible, so you can adapt it to your situation.

The six lessons can be covered in six sessions. We suggest that you (and your group) adopt a pace with which you are comfortable. If some lessons need more time than one group meeting, please allow for that. It may be that at times during the study, the Holy Spirit will lead you to slow down and even dwell on a point of significant impact for you or those with whom you are studying.

Self-Paced Bible Study

Each lesson has been divided into four parts so you can study it over a period of several days. Since each part includes a study of God's Word and a time for prayer and interacting with God, you may want to use this as your daily devotional guide. The Bible study has several features.

Scripture Reading. In Part 1 of each lesson, you'll be given an assignment to read or listen to a portion of Scripture. There may be more than one passage listed. It is best to begin your study with reading the key passages listed there. When studying the Bible, the best place to begin is with reading the Bible! That seems simple enough, but at times people read about the Bible rather than read the Bible itself. Start with the text and then proceed to the lesson itself. Audio versions of the Bible are available at Christian bookstores. You might prefer listening to the passage being read. You might even want to listen to it several times during the course while driving in your car or at some other time. We encourage you to read or listen to all of Genesis 37–50.

Throughout the workbook, key Scripture texts and, at times, entire passages are provided for you to read. This is to save you time in your study. We know many people don't take time to look up Bible verses that are only referenced. We want you to read God's Word because God uses it to speak to you. The Bible verses are the most important words in this book. As you read verses that are especially meaningful to you, you may want to turn to them in your Bible and underline them for future reference.

Interactives. Woven throughout the lessons are questions and statements intended to help you interact with God. The purpose of these questions is to help you apply the Word of God to your life today. These questions are marked with an arrow ▶. Some will be discussion questions that you can use with a small group. Others will be very personal, not intended for sharing in an open group. There may not be an obvious answer to the question, either. At times you will be instructed to read a section aloud, and at other times you will be encouraged to pause right then to pray 🙏.

Use these interactives to help you take what you have learned and apply it to your life. That is one of the unique strengths of this approach to Bible study. It helps you learn the lesson and think through how to live it. If you just read through this material and don't take time to interact with God, the information will be of little help to you. We don't want you just to know about God; we want you to experience Him in a dynamic and personal relationship. Do not neglect the times for prayer, both as an individual and in a small group. Spending time with Him in prayer will be a key part of your experience.

Main Column and Margin. The primary column for your study is the wide one on the right side of each page. Always start reading and studying in that column. Read through the lesson. It is a good practice to read with a highlighter pen to mark key words, phrases, or sentences.

The left margin will be a place for references. Key texts will be listed there. Occasionally we'll place an important statement or illustration in the margin.

Small-Group Bible Study

A Christian who was a part of the early church in Jerusalem would have had both large-group and small-group experiences. Both Acts 2 and 5 refer to the fact that the believers met together in the temple courts and from house to house.

"Every day they continued to meet together in the temple courts. They broke bread in their homes and ate together with glad and sincere hearts, praising God and enjoying the favor of all the people. And the Lord added to their number daily those who were being saved" (Acts 2:46–47).

"Day after day, in the temple courts and from house to house, they never stopped teaching and proclaiming the good news that Jesus is the Christ" (Acts 5:42).

Worship services in a local church today are large-group experiences like the early church had in the temple courts. The early church's small-group experiences took place in homes. Today, many people are involved in small groups for study of the Word and building relationships with other believers.

Small groups may be called a variety of names and may be structured in a variety of ways. A list of small-group opportunities includes, but is not limited to, Sunday school class, discipleship class, home Bible study group, cell group, midweek Bible study, and men's or women's ministry group.

This study guide is designed to be flexible enough that an individual or study group can use it. It would even work well as a tool for family devotions.

The following are some suggestions for using this guide effectively in a small group.

Leadership. We recommend that each group have a leader and, if possible, a leader apprentice or coleader. The apprentice is learning how to lead and is available to fill in if the leader is unable to attend a meeting. A coleader could be an apprentice or could be another individual who shares the leadership of the group or is the substitute leader when needed.

A leader does not have to be a content expert. Nor does a leader need to have studied through the entire workbook before beginning to lead, either. All members will study the content of this workbook in preparation for the meetings.

Group Size. Since the purpose of the small group is to allow for close relationships between believers, the group can't grow too large without hindering spiritual intimacy. A group that reaches 16-20 in regular attendance is probably ready to multiply.

Leading a Small-Group Meeting

The following suggestions will help the leaders of a small-group Bible study.

Plan how you will use your time. People appreciate knowing that their time will be used wisely, so set in advance your basic schedule. It may be that you will begin with refreshments, move to the study, and conclude with prayer. Some prefer to start the study time first and then allow for refreshments and extended fellowship time after. The Small-Group Meeting guide at the end of each lesson will help you progress through the lesson as a group. It goes through the same basic steps each week, though

you can deviate from it to meet the needs of your group.

Work at building relationships. One of the joys of being a disciple is fellowship with others. Be sure that all members are introduced by name to the group. Any visitors or new members should be welcomed. Sharing some basic information, such as place of employment or special interests, can help people get to know one another.

Commit to the small group. Some people find it a special blessing or benefit to have a formal group covenant. One is included in this book. It is a way of saying, "Count on me." It also means that the group is saying, "We will be there for you." If someone is missing, make contact with him or her. Do not assume the reason for the absence. You may be able to help with a problem that kept that person from attending. Also, you may become aware of a need. Perhaps God will enable the group to minister to that person at that time.

How to Use the Small-Group Meeting Guides

At the end of each chapter you will find a page to assist the leader(s) of the group. It outlines the basic format for each small-group meeting. Feel free to adjust the format to best fit your group. If you need to take more than one session together to work on a lesson, then allow the extra time. Do not rush just to complete the book in six weeks. Take the time needed to learn the lessons God has for you.

The first two activities in the meeting guides are fellowship-oriented. Begin with prayer and then work on building your relationships with one another.

The Reviewing the Lesson section is important. It will help you go back through the text of this workbook. It is vital for each member of the group to have the account from the Bible clearly in mind. While we are eager to see how the lesson applies to our lives, we must begin with the Word. Once that is clearly in mind, we can then move on to application.

The next part of the guide is Applying the Truths to Life. This is where the leader is most involved in shaping the time with the group. Look over the interactive questions. Time will probably not allow for your group to discuss all of them. Encourage the group members to work through all the interactives during the week. Then, during your time together, choose ones you think are most appropriate to discuss together.

Finally, use your time together to build fellowship and reach out to others. Specific suggestions are given in each lesson for activities that will enable this. Sharing refreshments at the beginning or end of your meeting can aid in the building of relationships. Encourage everyone to contribute in this aspect of your group fellowship. This will help keep the provision and preparation of food from being a burden to one and allow every member to feel that they have a part in the group.

Back to the Bible Resources

Back to the Bible began in 1939 primarily as a radio Bible-teaching ministry. To continue leading people into a dynamic relationship with God, the ministry has expanded to include the publication of resources for use with small groups. These small-group Bible studies are being developed as a service to the local church to help you experience the full dimensions of being a healthy Body of Christ.

Workbooks should be available through your local Christian bookstores. Any bookstore, however, can carry them. If you don't have a Christian bookstore, work with a local bookseller to stock the books for you and other Christians in your area. They can use the ISBN information on the back of this workbook to order them. If they should have difficulty, encourage them to contact Back to the Bible Publishing at 1-888-559-7878. Since you will need larger-than-normal quantities, place your order several weeks in advance of your planned starting time. If you prefer, you may order directly from Back to the Bible by calling 1-800-759-2425 or by visiting our Web site (www.resources.backtothebible.org). There you also can learn about other available resources and of new products to be released soon.

Sold Out by God

Genesis 37

When you hear the name "Joseph," what comes to mind? If you first heard the story of Joseph as a child—particularly in Sunday school—you probably think of his "coat of many colors." And even if you missed the Sunday school experience as a youngster, you probably have heard of the popular musical written by playwright Andrew Lloyd Webber entitled *Joseph and the Amazing Technicolor Dream Coat.*

However, once you've studied Joseph's life in-depth, you will probably always think first of his incredible trust in the faithfulness of God. His life is often identified as a "Romans 8:28 experience." He believed that God was sovereign in his life and had allowed his terrible experience in Egypt to achieve a divine purpose, even though he also understood that his brothers had acted in a sinful and evil way. The series of painful experiences Joseph went through prepared him for his own unique moment in history to fulfill God's purpose in his life. His own words (found in Genesis 50:20), spoken near the end of his life, show that he understood all he experienced was according to God's plan.

A close examination of Joseph's life also reveals an astounding commitment to integrity. That word comes from the Latin *integritas,* which means "soundness," and speaks of something as being whole or complete. Integrity is a moral quality. A person of integrity lives an honest and upright life.

A person of integrity also can be described as WYSIWYG—what you see is what you get. What he is on the outside is what he is on the inside—all the time. The events of life do not become excuses for sin or disobedience. In Potiphar's house, Pharaoh's prison, and even the palace, Joseph maintained his integrity and, in an interesting way, tested the integrity of his brothers.

► 1. **We are confronted with integrity issues daily. When we examine the subject of integrity, as Warren Wiersbe says, "it is not an autopsy on somebody else's corpse." Identify specific ways your integrity is challenged:**

Romans 8:28

"And we know that in all things God works for the good of those who love him, who have been called according to his purpose."

At home, such as when paying bills or doing your taxes.

_____

At school, such as when asked about your homework.

_____

At work, such as when asked for a progress report on a project.

_____

At church, such as when someone asks about your walk with God.

_____

As we study the life of Joseph, these two themes—God's sovereignty and Joseph's integrity—will become increasingly evident to you. There is an important connection between the two. When we truly believe that God is sovereign, we will commit to living a life of integrity, trusting God for the outcomes. Joseph did that. He stayed true to God's plan, living a life of integrity every day.

It is much easier for us to read about the life of Joseph than it was for him to live it. We have "the rest of the story," as news commentator Paul Harvey likes to say, but Joseph didn't. When you read the initial part of his story, remember that he did not know what the end would be. At the time he must have felt like God had sold him out.

▶ **2. The two themes we are studying are integrity and sovereignty. God is sovereign and we must live lives of integrity. Sometimes sovereignty does not tell us what the end will be. Does God have to tell us what His plan is for your life? Explain.**

_____

_____

_____

In this lesson we will begin to learn an interesting truth: *Sometimes what seems to be the worst turns out to be the best.* As we will see, Joseph had what seemed to be the best. He was the favored son to whom God had revealed a special plan for his life. Then the best quickly became what seemed to be the worst.

PART 1: Interacting with the Scripture

Reading/Hearing God's Word

► 3. Read or listen to the passages of Scripture listed in the margin. As you begin, ask God to speak to you through His Word. Watch for verses or ideas that are especially meaningful to you today. Once you finish, check the box indicating the passage(s) you read or listened to.

Meditating on God's Word

► 4. Now write a brief summary of a meaningful verse or idea you noticed.

_____

_____

_____

Understanding God's Word

► 5. Read again the focal passage for this week's lesson in the margin (Gen. 37:1–11). Underline any key words or phrases that seem especially meaningful to you.

► 6. Look back at these verses. Circle one of the underlined words or phrases that you would like to understand or experience more fully.

Looking through the Scripture to God

 Now pause to pray. "God, You are the sovereign of the universe. Help me to acknowledge that You know what is best for me. In times of difficulty and confusion, help me trust You and Your plan for my life. May I stay faithful to You and Your Word."

The old Sears catalog would sometimes give the buyer three options: good, better, and best. The "good" would be fine, but most people would prefer the "better" and want the "best." It's the same with life. At the very least we want the "good" life, hope for a "better" life, and dream about the "best."

When reality sets in, however, we realize that sometimes even the "good" is elusive. Or so we think. As we see things from our limited

---

Read or Listen to:

☐ Genesis 37:1–11

☐ Genesis 37:12–36

Genesis 37:1–11

"Jacob lived in the land where his father had stayed, the land of Canaan. This is the account of Jacob.

"Joseph, a young man of seventeen, was tending the flocks with his brothers, the sons of Bilhah and the sons of Zilpah, his father's wives, and he brought their father a bad report about them.

"Now Israel loved Joseph more than any of his other sons, because he had been born to him in his old age; and he made a richly ornamented robe for him. When his brothers saw that their father loved him more than any of them, they hated him and could not speak a kind word to him.

(continued on next page)

"Joseph had a dream, and when he told it to his brothers, they hated him all the more. He said to them, 'Listen to this dream I had: We were binding sheaves of grain out in the field when suddenly my sheaf rose and stood upright, while your sheaves gathered around mine and bowed down to it.'

"His brothers said to him, 'Do you intend to reign over us? Will you actually rule us?' And they hated him all the more because of his dream and what he had said.

"Then he had another dream, and he told it to his brothers. 'Listen,' he said, 'I had another dream, and this time the sun and moon and eleven stars were bowing down to me.'

"When he told his father as well as his brothers, his father rebuked him and said, 'What is this dream you had? Will your mother and I and your brothers actually come and bow down to the ground before you?' His brothers were jealous of him, but his father kept the matter in mind."

perspective, things may appear to be bad. But from a biblical perspective we learn that sometimes the worst may be the best! In Joseph's case, what seemed to be the best became the worst. Ultimately, however, he realized that the worst was for the best.

PART 2: The Royal Treatment of Joseph (Gen. 37:1-11)

At the tender age of 17, Joseph had both position and promise. One could say of his situation, "It doesn't get any better than this." Let's look at how life was good for him.

Joseph's Position—Favored Son (v. 3)

Jacob loved his son Joseph more than any of his 11 other sons. The reason given was that Joseph "had been born to him in his old age" (v. 3). Undoubtedly Jacob knew that his favoritism could cause friction in the family. He of all people would know since he had been favored by his mother over his twin brother, Esau. How could he forget all the trouble that caused!

In understanding Jacob's parental favoritism, we must not forget Rachel. She was the woman whom Jacob really loved. Joseph was the first son born as a result of deep love and affection rather than a mere physical act leading to procreation.

His birth had brought happiness to Rachel. For years she tried to have a child; for years she felt animosity toward Leah because of her sister's fertility. Finally, God opened her womb. When Joseph was born she cried out, "God has taken away my disgrace" (Gen. 30:23).

Now Rachel was dead. She had died about a year earlier. Perhaps Jacob transferred his love and esteem to this young son.

Joseph's favored position was made obvious by the gift of a very special coat. Some translators call this gift "a coat of many colors." However, it was far more than a typical garment with a few added touches of finery. The sleeves reached to the wrists and the main body of the coat to the ankles. It was beautifully tailored and decorated.

This was not the kind of coat worn by a shepherd who needs freedom of movement in both his arms and legs. Jacob never intended the coat to be functional. Rather, it represented Joseph's favored position in the family. It let everyone know that Joseph would be treated as Jacob's firstborn with all the rights and privileges—namely, that he was entitled to a double portion of the inheritance and would be the one to carry on the leadership of the family.

► 7. How has living in a culture of affluence affected your acceptance of difficulties? Specific situations you can discuss include:

Physical suffering, in an age of instant pain relievers and advanced medical treatment.

_____

_____

_____

Financial difficulties, when surrounded by people experiencing prosperity and success.

_____

_____

_____

Relationship failures, when problems are solved in a 30-minute television program but yours are ongoing.

_____

_____

_____

Life was good for Joseph, but it got even better.

Joseph's Promise—Future Ascendancy (vv. 6–7, 9)

Youthful dreams are a part of growing up. It is not unusual for a 17-year-old to have dreams of what life might be like. For Joseph, however, there was a special significance to his dreams. They were a revelation from God.

The scene of the first dream was agricultural. Joseph dreamed of a time in which he and his brothers were binding sheaves of grain. His "sheaf rose and stood upright, while [theirs] gathered around [Joseph's] and bowed down to it" (v. 7). The interpretation was obvious—but not so the implication. Clearly, the dream revealed Joseph in a position of authority. But it wasn't clear then that his authority would come at a time of famine when his brothers would travel to Egypt to seek his assistance.

The scene of the second dream was celestial. Again the interpretation was obvious. The 11 stars represented his brothers, and the sun and moon represented his parents.

When Joseph told his father the dreams, Jacob immediately understood their message. He rebuked Joseph and asked, "Will your mother and I and your brothers actually come and bow down to the ground before you?" (v. 10). Jacob had already bowed to his brother (Gen. 33:3). Now he was being told of a day when the entire family would bow to his son. He intended Joseph to be favored, but perhaps not that favored!

▶ 8. James 1:19 tells us that "everyone should be . . . slow to speak." Looking back on this scene, we may think Joseph could have avoided alienating his family by keeping quiet. Are there times when it would be better not to speak? Read Proverbs 10:19 and 17:28 in the margin.

Proverbs 10:19

"When words are many, sin is not absent, but he who holds his tongue is wise."

Proverbs 17:28

"Even a fool is thought wise if he keeps silent, and discerning if he holds his tongue."

_____

_____

_____

You may wonder why Joseph told his family his dreams. Some people think Joseph had a problem with pride. Others suggest that in his youthful naiveté he did not realize the potential for stirring up hatred and resentment in his brothers. What we do know is that while the brothers became upset, the Scriptures do not condemn Joseph for revealing these prophecies.

For Joseph, the present and the future looked good. He had position and promise. Everything appeared to be working in his favor. But soon it would look like everything had turned against him.

PART 3: The Resentment of Joseph by His Brothers (Gen. 37:1-11)

It's easy to predict the results of Jacob's favoritism toward Joseph and of Joseph's sharing his dreams. His brothers despised him so much that they "could not speak a kind word to him" (v. 4). From the text we can identify three basic reasons for their resentment.

They resented him for his report (v. 2)

Joseph was tending the flocks with his half-brothers. He was the youngest of the brothers; perhaps, as Stuart Briscoe writes, "he was an assistant to these men who themselves did not rank very high in the family pecking order."[1] At any rate, Joseph did not help the relationship by bringing "a bad report" about them to their father.

We are not told the content of the report, but we can certainly speculate it must have been a serious violation of God's standards of righteousness. From Joseph's "bad report," Jacob had reason to wonder about his sons' behavior.

They resented him for his robe (v. 4)

The beautiful robe was a visible reminder to his older brothers that Joseph was the favored one. He, not any of them, would be in charge and receive the inheritance of the firstborn. Scripture does speak of Joseph as "prince among his brothers" (Deut. 33:16) and notes that he received "the rights of the firstborn" (1 Chron. 5:2).

Their response is understandable. It's easy to see how this treatment of Joseph would threaten and anger his carnal brothers. Even if they had been spiritual men, this would seem unfair. Their resentment was intense. Joseph must have been aware of their anger, even though it appears that Jacob was not.

They resented him for his revelations (v. 8)

Eventually Joseph would become a very wise man after learning many lessons in the school of hard knocks. At this point in his life, however, he was definitely naïve. After all, he was only 17. His heart was pure, but he lacked the experience and wisdom that comes with age.

He made a serious error in judgment when he shared his dreams with his brothers. They were already in bondage to their jealousy and hatred, so relating his dreams was like waving a red blanket in front of a charging bull—in this case, 11 "bulls." Their intense negative reactions were predictable. Even Jacob was shocked by what he heard when Joseph told him the second dream.

Jealousy and hatred are withering emotions that are devastating to human relationships, particularly within families. Generally speaking, people who resent others find it very difficult to communicate positively with those who are the object of their resentment. And this was exactly what happened in Joseph's family. His brothers were not about to compliment Joseph, nor were they going to wish him God's best.

▶ **9. When hate is in the heart it usually appears on the tongue. Read the verses from Proverbs 27 and 29 in the margin and answer this question: What would you say to the brothers?**

_____

_____

_____

Proverbs 27:4

"Anger is cruel and fury overwhelming, but who can stand before jealousy?"

Proverbs 29:10–11

"Bloodthirsty men hate a man of integrity and seek to kill the upright.

"A fool gives full vent to his anger, but a wise man keeps himself under control."

One-on-one hatred is difficult to deal with. But this problem is compounded and greatly complicated when people are drawn together in common hatred. They feed on one another's feelings of resentment and collaborate in their actions. They spur one another on. This is exactly what happened among Joseph's brothers.

Song of Solomon 8:6, KJV

"Jealousy is cruel as the grave: the coals thereof are coals of fire, which hath a most vehement flame."

▶ **10. Read Song of Solomon 8:6 in the margin. Why is jealousy compared to coals of fire?**

_____

_____

_____

PART 4: The Revenge of Joseph's Brothers (Gen. 37:12–36)

About the only way to explain what happens next is to say that Jacob was out of touch with his own family. He was so unaware of the simmering rage of his sons that he put Joseph into a very dangerous situation. The brothers must have hid their rancor well, for neither their words nor deeds had let their father know how intense their hatred was for the son he loved so much.

▶ **11. Jacob is repeatedly portrayed in Genesis as a passive father. How is this lack of reaction seen in the following settings?**

His reaction to news of Dinah's rape (34:5).

_____

_____

His reaction to Joseph's bad report about his brothers (37:2).

_____

_____

His reaction to the news that Simeon was in prison in Egypt (42:36).

_____

_____

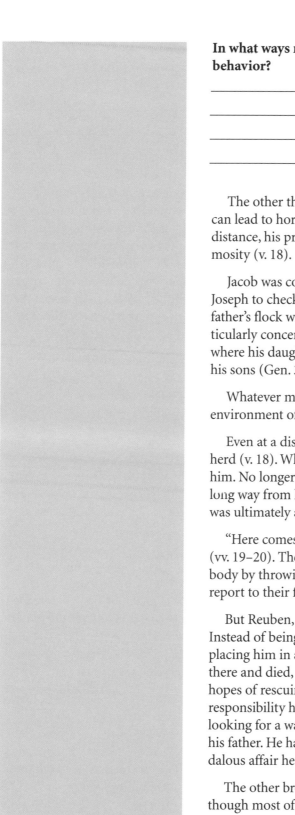

In what ways might his passivity have contributed to his sons' behavior?

_____

_____

_____

_____

The other thing to consider at this point is how hatred in the heart can lead to horrible actions. From the moment they saw Joseph in the distance, his presence served as the catalyst for acting out their animosity (v. 18).

Jacob was concerned about the welfare of his other sons, so he sent Joseph to check on them. The place where they were grazing their father's flock was at least 50 miles from home. Perhaps Jacob was particularly concerned because the location was near Shechem, the city where his daughter was raped and the men of the city killed by two of his sons (Gen. 34).

Whatever motivated Jacob to send him, Joseph moved from an environment of love and acceptance to one of hatred and rejection.

Even at a distance, Joseph looked like a prince, not a fellow shepherd (v. 18). When they saw him approaching, they plotted to kill him. No longer was he in the safety of his father's eye. Now he was a long way from home, out in the wilderness, in a place of danger. It was ultimately a danger of his brothers' design.

"Here comes that dreamer!" they said. "Come now, let's kill him" (vv. 19–20). They conspired to "take his life" and to dispose of his body by throwing him into one of the cisterns. They would then report to their father that a "ferocious animal" had "devoured" Joseph.

But Reuben, the oldest brother, came up with an alternative plan. Instead of being directly responsible for Joseph's death, he suggested placing him in a cistern. Then it would look like Joseph had fallen in there and died, unable to escape. In reality, Reuben suggested this in hopes of rescuing Joseph later. Perhaps Reuben was thinking of the responsibility he had as the oldest son. Or it could be that he was looking for a way to restore communication and a relationship with his father. He had been out of favor with Jacob ever since the scandalous affair he had had with Bilhah, Jacob's concubine (Gen. 35:22).

The other brothers consented to Reuben's alternate plan even though most of them still wanted to take Joseph's life. But they definitely agreed on one thing—they hated Joseph and loathed the idea of having him in authority over them. Consequently, when Joseph arrived, they tore off his richly ornamented robe and "threw him into the cistern" (v. 24).

▶ **12. Compare this scene with Proverbs 1:10–11, 15–16 (in the margin). What important lesson do you learn in regard to "going along with the crowd"?**

_____

_____

_____

You can imagine Joseph's shock and fear as he walked into this threatening situation. In his naiveté, he must have thought his brothers would be happy to see him. Though the immediate text does not specify Joseph's emotional response, we know from the brothers' later confession in Egypt that he was extremely "distressed." He "pleaded" with them "for his life." However, they showed no mercy and "would not listen" (Gen. 42:21). So intense was their hatred for him that their horrible act did not even diminish their appetite. Instead, "they sat down to eat their meal" (v. 25).

Just then the plan changed. Judah proposed a profitable alternative. "Let's sell him to the Ishmaelites and not lay our hands on him" (v. 27). The brothers agreed and for 20 shekels of silver sold Joseph to a passing caravan of merchants.

Joseph ultimately found himself in a country and culture he didn't know, hearing a language he didn't understand. Hardened slave traders were now transporting him. One day he was set on the block and sold like a cheap piece of merchandise. The highest bidder was a man name Potiphar, who was one of Pharaoh's officials, the captain of the guard (v. 36).

The best truly had become the worst.

During the intervening years, Jacob felt the pain of his loss. His sons returned home with Joseph's robe, which they had doctored with the blood of a goat to deceive their father. (It is an interesting twist of irony to remember that Jacob had deceived his father with a meal made of goat meat, according to Genesis 27:9). So great was Jacob's agony that he would later declare, "Everything is against me!" (Gen. 42:36). In reality, God in His sovereignty was at work for his ultimate good.

The same was true for Joseph. He who was once the favored son was now a slave. He who was given a vision of future ascendancy now was bought by the highest bidder. In his heart he must have felt the pain of being sold by his brothers and sold out by God.

Many years would pass before Joseph would not only know but also live the rest of the story. The day would come when he would say to his brothers, "You intended to harm me, but God intended it for good" (Gen. 50:20).

John 14:1–3

"'Do not let your hearts be troubled. Trust in God; trust also in me. In my Father's house are many rooms; if it were not so, I would have told you. I am going there to prepare a place for you. And if I go and prepare a place for you, I will come back and take you to be with me that you also may be where I am.'"

Romans 8:18–21

"I consider that our present sufferings are not worth comparing with the glory that will be revealed in us. The creation waits in eager expectation for the sons of God to be revealed. For the creation was subjected to frustration, not by its own choice, but by the will of the one who subjected it, in hope that the creation itself will be liberated from its bondage to decay and brought into the glorious freedom of the children of God."

2 Corinthians 5:1–2

"Now we know that if the earthly tent we live in is destroyed, we have a building from God, an eternal house in heaven, not built by human hands. Meanwhile we groan, longing to be clothed with our heavenly dwelling."

▶ **13. There is great value for the Christian to stay focused on the future without losing sight of the present. How is this demonstrated in the following verses?**

John 14:1–3

_____

_____

_____

Romans 8:18–21

_____

_____

_____

2 Corinthians 5:1–2

_____

_____

_____

We can read Joseph's entire story in just a few chapters of Scripture. But for him, his "best-to-worst-to-best" life unfolded slowly over many years. Through it all, however, there is no condemnation of the young man who stayed true to God's plan, even in the darkest of situations.

Even when the best becomes the worst, God wants us to remember that He is the sovereign of the universe. Ultimately He will accomplish His greatest good in our lives. Remembering that God is in control enables us to emerge from any situation better, not bitter.

Small-Group Meeting 1

Opening Prayer

Begin each time with prayer. Ask God to bless your time of study together as you seek to understand the lessons from the life of Joseph and apply them to your own life.

Building Relationships

Each of the "Building Relationships" suggestions may tie in with the lesson you are studying or a previous one, using some aspect of it to give group members an opportunity to get to know each other better. This activity especially helps everyone get to know more about the spiritual lives of the people in the group. Since the emphasis of Lesson 1 is on the sovereignty of God, ask two or three people to tell about a time when they realized that God had been at work in a particular situation in their lives.

Reviewing the Lesson

1. Remind the group of the two themes that are found in the life of Joseph: God's sovereignty and Joseph's integrity. Ask, "Why do you think that the sovereignty of God encourages us to live a life of integrity?" (See the first paragraph after #1 on page 10.) Help the group understand that our responsibility is always to do right and trust God for the outcomes.

2. Review the three major sections of this lesson—The Royal Treatment of Joseph, The Resentment of Joseph's Brothers, and The Revenge of Joseph's Brothers. The broad picture of what happens in this lesson needs to be clear in each person's mind. Ask, "What are some things that you noticed in this lesson that were new to you?"

3. For what three reasons did Joseph's brothers resent him? (See Part 3 beginning on page 14.)

Applying the Truths to Life

Select interactive questions to discuss as a group. Some are intended for personal reflection and are not for sharing with the group. Be careful to choose ones that are for open discussion. Include some from each of the four parts of the lesson.

Significant ones to include in this discussion are #2

(page 10), #7 (page 13), #8 (page 14), #11 (page 16), and #12 (page 18).

Read aloud the verses printed in the margin on page 19. Then discuss each passage based on your answers to #13.

Ministering to One Another

One of the special blessings of being part of a small group is that you can be aware of one another's needs. As has been said, it is noticed if someone is missing and it is known if someone has a need. Be sure to make contact with any who miss a meeting. Also be prepared to help one another with their needs, whether they need practical help, emotional support, or spiritual instruction.

Reaching Out to Others

You need to decide if your group is an "open" or a "closed" group. Closed groups do not allow others to join after the first few times together. This allows for the group to develop more openness in what is shared.

An open group intends for others to join at any time. If yours is an open group, be sure all understand that. In addition, take time in your first meeting to think of what you can do specifically to get others to come to your meetings. Every time your group meets, set an extra chair in the room as a reminder to invite someone to join and sit in that seat.

Closing Prayer Time

Distribute sheets of paper that can be used to write down prayer requests. Encourage everyone to keep these with their study guides and bring them to every group meeting. Also remember to use these during private prayer between group meetings. As the group grows more familiar with one another and develops greater trust that confidences will be kept, the requests will become more specific. Remind everyone of the importance of keeping confidences. These prayer times will help the group discover opportunities to minister to one another.

The leader should let everyone know who will close the prayer time.

Do Right

Genesis 39

In view of the declining values in our society, this segment of Joseph's life is probably one of the most relevant to our lives. We live at a time when sexual immorality is both assumed and accepted. Movies, television programs, and books treat instances of immorality as normal. Then there are the situations we know about personally. These may involve well-known people whose sexual activities become news stories. Or they may involve close friends who give in to sexual temptation. In some cases, their immorality has destroyed their families.

Acts of immorality should serve as a wake-up call. They should startle us every time they happen and make us realize how weak most of us are in this area.

Dr. Bob Jones Sr., the evangelist from the first half of the 20th century who founded Bob Jones University, was known for his chapel sayings. In a sentence or two he could communicate in a memorable way an important principle for Christian living. One of his sayings that especially applies to this lesson is, "Do right even if the stars fall."

Joseph certainly was enticed to do wrong. Potiphar's wife repeatedly attempted to seduce him, but he never gave in. Instead, he did what was right. And in a sense, the stars did fall—doing right landed him in prison.

We can learn three outstanding lessons from the narrative in Genesis 39. The first and most obvious one is in regard to overcoming sexual temptation. Joseph successfully resisted the advances of Potiphar's wife. The second lesson concerns the faithfulness of God. As you read the chapter, notice the number of times it says "the Lord was with Joseph." The third lesson is the importance of maintaining integrity at all times, at all cost. Knowing that God will always be faithful encourages us to be people of integrity, helping each of us overcome sexual temptation.

Read or Listen to:

☐ Genesis 39:1–6

☐ Genesis 39:7–20

PART 1: Interacting with the Scripture

Reading/Hearing God's Word

▶ **1. Read or listen to the passages of Scripture listed in the margin. Ask God to speak to you through His Word. Watch for verses or ideas that are especially meaningful to you today. Once you finish, check the box indicating the passage(s) you read or listened to.**

Meditating on God's Word

▶ **2. Write a brief summary of a meaningful verse or idea you just noticed.**

_____

_____

_____

Understanding God's Word

▶ **3. Read again the focal passage for this week's lesson in the margin (Gen. 39:2–12). Underline any key words or phrases that seem especially meaningful to you.**

▶ **4. Look back at these verses. Circle one of the underlined words or phrases that you would like to understand or experience more fully.**

Looking through the Scripture to God

Genesis 39:2–12

"The LORD was with Joseph and he prospered, and he lived in the house of his Egyptian master. When his master saw that the LORD was with him and that the LORD gave him success in everything he did, Joseph found favor in his eyes and became his attendant. Potiphar put him in charge of his household, and he entrusted to his care everything he owned. From the time he put him in charge of his household and of all that he owned, the LORD blessed the household of the Egyptian because of Joseph. The blessing of the LORD was on everything Potiphar had, both in the house and in the field. So he left in

 Now pause to pray. "Faithful Father, I live in a world of temptation to sexual sins. Help me learn from this lesson that while immorality is accepted and expected by so many, Your Word says it is wrong. Help me learn to trust Your faithfulness in times of temptation. May I by Your grace live a life of sexual integrity that pleases You and honors those around me."

(continued on next page)

Joseph's care everything he had; with Joseph in charge, he did not concern himself with anything except the food he ate.

"Now Joseph was well-built and handsome, and after a while his master's wife took notice of Joseph and said, 'Come to bed with me!'

"But he refused. 'With me in charge,' he told her, 'my master does not concern himself with anything in the house; everything he owns he has entrusted to my care. No one is greater in this house than I am. My master has withheld nothing from me except you, because you are his wife. How then could I do such a wicked thing and sin against God?' And though she spoke to Joseph day after day, he refused to go to bed with her or even be with her.

"One day he went into the house to attend to his duties, and none of the household servants was inside. She caught him by his cloak and said, 'Come to bed with me!' But he left his cloak in her hand and ran out of the house."

PART 2: The Faithfulness of God to Joseph (Gen. 39:1–6)

The caravan headed to Egypt, taking Joseph far from family and familiar surroundings. But no matter how far it traveled, it could never take him away from God's faithfulness. In the midst of this discouragement we find what is most encouraging—God never forsook Joseph.

Apart from his prophetic dreams, Joseph had no clue as to what would happen to him. However, after years of painful suffering, he would discover that God had a special place for him in the unique and turbulent history of His chosen people. But Joseph could not occupy that place until he was adequately prepared, both spiritually and emotionally. Though the Lord was preparing him during his younger years, his intensive preparation began in Egypt.

Potiphar's Purchase (v. 1)

When the Midianite merchants arrived in Egypt, they sold Joseph to Potiphar, a high-ranking Egyptian official who is identified in Scripture as "captain of the guard" (v. 1). In other words, Potiphar was the lead man in Pharaoh's team of bodyguards, which means the king of Egypt placed his total trust in him. The Hebrew word translated "guard" can mean "executioner." Therefore, as captain of the guard, it also was Potiphar's responsibility to implement the death penalty for criminal behavior. He was indeed a prominent man in Egypt.

God's Presence (v. 2)

Joseph's brothers may have forgotten about the brother they had so cruelly sold into slavery, but Joseph's God did not! Repeatedly in this chapter we read that "the LORD was with Joseph" (v. 2) and that "the LORD gave him success" (v. 3).

The specific word that is used five times in verses 2–6 is *Yahweh*. Sometimes this word is translated "Jehovah," which is actually not a word. Rather than take the name of the Lord in vain, the Hebrews would write the consonants for *Yahweh* but put in the vowels from *Adonai*, which means "lord." The closest possible pronunciation of the resulting word is "Jehovah." English versions of the Bible are careful to note this particular word by using all capital letters. It is a special name for God, one that reminds us that He is the dependable and faithful God. When you see "LORD" in the Bible, it is this word.

Joseph's story is about the faithfulness of God. The Lord truly was with him. At that uncertain moment, his future hanging in a balance, he appeared to be alone, but he was not. The Bible leaves us no doubt about God's presence.

Deuteronomy 31:6

"'Be strong and courageous. Do not be afraid or terrified because of them, for the LORD your God goes with you; he will never leave you nor forsake you.'"

Matthew 28:20

"'And teaching them to obey everything I have commanded you. And surely I am with you always, to the very end of the age.'"

Hebrews 13:5

"Keep your lives free from the love of money and be content with what you have, because God has said, 'Never will I leave you; never will I forsake you.'"

▶ **5. Do you ever doubt God's presence? Have you ever experienced a time when it felt like God had deserted you? What encouragement can you draw from the following verses?**

Deuteronomy 31:6

_____

_____

Matthew 28:20

_____

_____

Hebrews 13:5

_____

_____

Joseph Prospered (vv. 3–6)

We're not told anything about Joseph's first duties. But his character and faithfulness eventually became obvious to Potiphar. What he did, he did well. What then happened to Joseph is a graphic and powerful illustration of what Jesus taught His disciples hundreds of years later— a servant who has "been faithful with a few things" will be put "in charge of many things" (Matt. 25:21). That is exactly what happened to this young slave.

This high-ranking official recognized that Joseph was no ordinary man. In fact, Joseph had such an outstanding testimony that Potiphar, who worshiped the "gods" of Egypt, came to understand that Joseph served a very special God. More specifically, Potiphar concluded that "the LORD was with him and that the LORD gave him success in everything he did"(v. 3). The source of Joseph's success without doubt was the Lord.

▶ **6. Potiphar "noticed" Joseph because:**

☐ He was well-built and handsome, or

☐ The Lord was with him.

In light of your answer, what truths can you learn about the importance of your character? (Read 1 Samuel 16:7 in the margin.)

_____

_____

_____

Joseph Promoted (vv. 4–6)

Joseph's behavior was so outstanding and above reproach that he became Potiphar's executive assistant. This man of power and wealth entrusted to his care "everything he owned" (v. 4). This meant supervising all the other servants and employees, overseeing Potiphar's finances, and administering his agricultural interests and all of his other business activities. In fact, Potiphar "did not concern himself with anything except the food he ate" (v. 6). In these verses the Hebrew word *kol*, which literally means "all," is used repeatedly to emphasize the all-encompassing nature of Potiphar's trust. "The completeness of Joseph's dedication to Potiphar, the completeness of Potiphar's trust in Joseph, and the completeness of the Lord's blessing on the household are underscored in this unity by the five-fold repetition of 'all'."[1]

► 7. Read the following statements about stewardship and then illustrate each point using Genesis 39:4–6a.

A steward is a manager, not an owner.

_____

_____

The owner entrusts the care of his/her possessions to the steward.

_____

_____

The steward is trusted completely and must be faithful.

_____

_____

Joseph's role as manager for Potiphar is an illustration of the biblical concept of stewardship. The master not only trusted the servant but also *entrusted* the steward with the management of the household. In the same way, God assigns us the responsibility to be stewards. We are not owners of anything but stewards of what belongs to God.

These verses demonstrate that God is faithful and in control, the sovereign of all. He had a plan for Joseph and would see it accomplished. It is not a minor point that the Hebrew word *Yahweh* is used for God. He is the dependable and faithful God who worked in Joseph's life and situation. He works in your life and situation as well.

PART 3: The Faithfulness of Joseph to God (Gen. 39:7–20)

Faithfulness is a two-way street. God's faithfulness is always certain. There is never a question as to whether or not He will be faithful. But our faithfulness, while expected by God, is the uncertain part. At the heart of our faithfulness is the responsibility to live a life of integrity. The wife of Joseph's master would put his integrity to the test.

Potiphar was not the only one who was taken with Joseph. Eventually, Potiphar's wife "took notice" of him as well (v. 7). He was, after all, "well-built and handsome" (v. 6). Her motives, however, were quite different from her husband's. While he saw Joseph as a valuable servant, she looked upon him as one to satisfy her desire for physical pleasure.

The Request of Potiphar's Wife (v. 7)

Potiphar's wife was anything but subtle. She did more looking than talking. Her proposition to Joseph was straightforward and direct. In the Hebrew language, it took only two words to say, "Come to bed with me!" (v. 7). Picture the scene: a young, unmarried, handsome man left alone with a woman offering him sex.

Temptation is a part of life. None of us is immune from it. Jesus Christ Himself was tempted. Regarding temptation, Dietrich Bonhoeffer wrote, "In our members there is a slumbering inclination towards desire which is both sudden and fierce. With irresistible power desire seizes mastery over the flesh. All at once a secret, smoldering fire is kindled. The flesh burns and is in flames. . . . The lust thus aroused envelops the mind and will of man in deepest darkness. The powers of clear discrimination and of decision are taken from us. . . . It is here that everything within me rises up against the Word of God."[2]

Proverbs 6:20–29

20 "My son, keep your father's commands and do not forsake your mother's teaching.

21 Bind them upon your heart forever; fasten them around your neck. 22 When you walk, they will guide you; when you sleep, they will watch over you; when you awake, they will speak to you. 23 For these commands are a lamp, this teaching is a light, and the corrections of discipline are the way to life, 24 keeping you from the immoral woman, from the smooth tongue of the wayward wife. 25 Do not lust in your heart after her beauty or let her captivate you with her eyes, 26 for the prostitute reduces you to a loaf of bread, and the adulteress preys upon your very life. 27 Can a man scoop fire into his lap without his clothes being burned? 28 Can a man walk on hot coals without his feet being scorched? 29 So is he who sleeps with another man's wife; no one who touches her will go unpunished."

Proverbs 7:21–23

21 "With persuasive words she led him astray; she seduced him with her smooth talk. 22 All at once he followed her like an ox going to the slaughter, like a deer stepping into a

(continued on next page)

What Joseph faced was an intense temptation. F. B. Meyer commented that "this was no ordinary temptation. Joseph was not a stone mummy, but a red-blooded young man in his late twenties. It was not one temptation on one day, but a repeated temptation.... An old story tells how when Joseph began to talk about God to the temptress, she flung her skirt over the bust of the god that stood in the chamber and said, 'Now, God will not see.' But Joseph answered, 'My God sees!'"[3]

▶ **8. Read Proverbs 6:20–29 and 7:21–23 in the margin. While the world tries to make sexual immorality look desirable, God paints a darker picture. Note the things God says about it.**

Immorality reduces you to what (6:26)?

_____

What do you think that means?

_____

Is this a way of describing poverty?

_____

How is lust like fire (6:27)?

_____

Can you escape without being burned?

_____

Will adultery go unpunished (6:29)?

_____

What is Solomon saying through the examples of the ox, deer, and bird (7:22–23)?

_____

_____

_____

noose [23] till an arrow pierces his liver, like a bird darting into a snare, little knowing it will cost him his life."

Ultimately adultery cost this man what?

_____

_____

Joseph's Restraint (v. 8)

The response of Joseph was likewise simple and direct: "he refused" (v. 8). Potiphar's wife was, in many respects, Joseph's superior. He was her servant. In view of this, his resistance is remarkable!

Joseph's resistance to temptation is even more remarkable in view of this woman's persistence. Not only was her invitation direct, but she also kept after him "day after day" (v. 10). And we need not even speculate to conclude that her invitation was more than verbal. She would have used every visual seductive technique she could think of. But "day after day" Joseph "refused to go to bed with her or even be with her" (v. 10).

▶ **9. Joseph did not allow opportunity to get the best of him. To avoid the repeated attempts to seduce him, "he refused to . . . even be with her" (v. 10). What safeguards have you built to keep from temptations:**

At work?

_____

At home?

_____

At leisure?

_____

Remember, too, that Joseph's knowledge of God's laws was limited. This took place about 400 years before God thundered from Mount Sinai, "'You shall not commit adultery. . . . You shall not covet your neighbor's wife'" (Ex. 20:14, 17). But in spite of Joseph's limited knowledge of God's laws, in spite of his own natural desires and tendencies, and—perhaps most significant—in spite of the natural opportunity to cooperate in a relatively safe, secret setting, Joseph still resisted!

Proverbs 7:13–20

¹³ "She took hold of him and kissed him and with a brazen face she said: ¹⁴ 'I have fellowship offerings at home; today I fulfilled my vows. ¹⁵ So I came out to meet you; I looked for you and have found you! ¹⁶ I have covered my bed with colored linens from Egypt. ¹⁷ I have perfumed my bed with myrrh, aloes and cinnamon. ¹⁸ Come, let's drink deep of love till morning; let's enjoy ourselves with love! ¹⁹ My husband is not at home; he has gone on a long journey. ²⁰ He took his purse filled with money and will not be home till full moon.'"

▶ **10. In Proverbs 7:13–20, Solomon records the enticing words of an adulteress. How does she use the following to encourage immorality?**

Her religious acts (v. 14).

_____

_____

Her aggressive pursuit (v. 15).

_____

_____

Her bedroom (vv. 16–17).

_____

_____

Her promise of sexual pleasure (v. 18).

_____

_____

Her husband's absence (vv. 19–20).

_____

_____

Reasons for His Resistance (vv. 8b–10)

Joseph told Potiphar's wife there were two reasons why he would not go to bed with her. He knew that adultery was not only a "wicked thing" but also "a sin against God" (v. 9). His commitment to this solid principle was the basis of his action. He would not disobey God. Though he was limited in his knowledge of God's laws, he knew the Lord personally and believed in his heart that it would be wrong to engage in sexual relations with Potiphar's wife or any woman who was not his own wife. He had strong moral convictions; he would not allow himself to sin against God.

Proverbs 6:32–35

"But a man who commits adultery lacks judgment; whoever does so destroys himself. Blows and disgrace are his lot, and his shame will never be wiped away; for jealousy arouses a husband's fury, and he will show no mercy when he takes revenge. He will not accept any compensation; he will refuse the bribe, however great it is."

The other reason was his commitment to his position. Potiphar trusted Joseph so completely that he did not "concern himself with anything in the house" (v. 8). He entrusted Joseph with it all, and Joseph would not violate that trust.

▶ **11. Read Proverbs 6:32–35 in the margin. Below, list the four consequences of adultery found in these verses:**

a. _____

b. _____

c. _____

d. _____

Joseph Runs (vv. 11–12)

A day comes that is ideal in the mind of Potiphar's wife. Only two people are in the house: she and the object of her desire. She was an evil seductress, desiring sex with Joseph, willing to ignore his reasons for refusal, caring nothing about the trust between her husband and Joseph. Her only interest was in gratifying her sensual desires. Repeatedly she had tried and failed; now came the perfect opportunity. For all we know, this may have been a deliberate setup. In her mind every reason for Joseph to resist her advances was removed.

Being more aggressive than ever, she grabbed his cloak and pulled him in her direction. Joseph instantly resisted, pulling in the opposite direction. Her grip was firm, for he left her standing alone with his cloak in her hand as he literally "ran out of the house" (v. 12).

Prior to this aggressive approach, Joseph resisted graciously. After all, he was her servant. But this time there was no way he could do so. Her actions were overt and sudden. And so was Joseph's response. Intense sexual advances combined with outright rejection often generate intense hostility. This is exactly what happened. Her cries of rage could be heard outside the house.

► **12. When we determine to live a godly life, there will be times we say no and do not participate in some things others think are fine. How do people react when you have refused to:**

Participate in a betting pool at the office?

_____

Decline to stop at a bar?

_____

Refuse to "pad" an expense account?

_____

The Result: Prison (vv. 13–20)

Quickly and impulsively, Potiphar's wife twisted the story. Her lust turned to hatred. Screaming for her servants, she accused Joseph of attempted rape. When Potiphar came home, she repeated her twisted story, showing him Joseph's cloak to prove her point. The Scriptures state that Potiphar "burned with anger" and he immediately had Joseph imprisoned (vv. 19–20).

Joseph's only "crime" was that he was handsome and committed to live a life of integrity. He did not allow the events or circumstances of life to become an excuse for sin. The opportunity to sin and get away with it did not affect his integrity, either. Risking the wrath of his owner's wife and the possibility of prison, if not execution, did not sway him.

God was with Joseph, and he trusted God for every outcome. He stayed true to God's plan, living a life of integrity every day.

► **13. Read Genesis 39:21–23 in the margin. What four things did God do for Joseph in prison?**

a. _____

b. _____

c. _____

d. _____

Genesis 39:21–23

"The LORD was with him; he showed him kindness and granted him favor in the eyes of the prison warden. So the warden put Joseph in charge of all those held in the prison, and he was made responsible for all that was done there. The warden paid no attention to anything under Joseph's care, because the LORD was with Joseph and gave him success in whatever he did."

PART 4: Living a Life of Sexual Integrity

The situation described in Genesis 39 has been repeated countless times. Sexual immorality is not a thing of ancient history but of all history and of all times—including our own right now. Joseph maintained his sexual integrity and so must we. From this chapter we can learn several principles to help us keep our purity.

Principle 1. When we are the most successful, we are often the most vulnerable to sexual temptation.

How true this was in Joseph's case! Though caused by God's blessing, his success did not insulate him from Satan's attacks.

No matter what our success, we must be on guard in a particular way, for this is often when the enemy will strike. If Satan can catch us with our guard down, he may at that moment deliver a devastating blow. Before we know what has happened, we may find ourselves in a compromising situation, particularly if we yield to sin in some fashion. The apostle Paul stated it very directly to the Corinthians: "If you think you are standing firm, be careful that you don't fall!" (1 Cor. 10:12).

▶ **14. Read 1 Corinthians 10:13 in the margin. What does God promise to do to help us in times of temptation?**

_____

_____

_____

Principle 2. To resist temptation, we must have firm moral and ethical convictions based on a biblical value system.

Again, Joseph beautifully illustrates this principle. He was determined not to violate the trust Potiphar placed in him nor sin against God. In his heart and mind he knew he was accountable both to Potiphar and to God.

Human Accountability. The order of accountability here is very important. It moves from the human to the divine. There are people who trust us not to yield to temptation: our children, our spouses, our fellow Christians, and last but not least, many of our non-Christian friends and associates. Having firm convictions and desires not to violate their trust is a great source of strength. This is why having an accountability partner is so important. Such a person helps keep us from wrong by reminding us to do right. This works because

1 Corinthians 10:13

"No temptation has seized you except what is common to man. And God is faithful; he will not let you be tempted beyond what you can bear. But when you are temped, he will also provide a way out so that you can stand up under it."

we know that we have to tell him about our actions and answer to him. It does not work when we fail to be truthful and accepting of that person's counsel.

▶ **15. Satan would like us to think that our sin affects only ourselves, but this is not true. Joseph knew that if he sinned it would affect Potiphar. Read 2 Samuel 12:14 in the margin. What consequence of David's sin did Nathan point out?**

_____

_____

2 Samuel 12:14

"'But because by doing this you have made the enemies of the LORD show utter contempt, the son born to you will die.'"

Divine Accountability. The most important motivating source for not yielding to temptation should be our relationship with God. Joseph knew that and ultimately so did David after his sin with Bathsheba. He said to Nathan, "I have sinned against the LORD" (2 Sam. 12:13). Furthermore, the strongest deterrent ought to be based on His love and grace toward us, not our fear of what He might do or allow to happen to us if we sin. Certainly, fear of God's discipline should be a factor, but our primary motivation should be what Paul wrote to Titus:

"For the grace of God that brings salvation has appeared to all men. It teaches us to say 'No' to ungodliness and worldly passions, and to live self-controlled, upright and godly lives in this present age, while we wait for the blessed hope—the glorious appearing of our great God and Savior, Jesus Christ, who gave himself for us to redeem us from all wickedness and to purify for himself a people that are his very own, eager to do what is good" (Titus 2:11–14).

Principle 3. To resist temptation, we must avoid verbal and visual stimuli.

There is a phrase in Joseph's story that is easy to miss, and yet it is a key in overcoming temptation. Not only did Joseph consistently refuse the invitation from Potiphar's wife, but he also refused to "even be with her" (Gen. 39:10).

Many temptations are generated by verbal and visual stimuli. We can never avoid them all. To do so we would have to leave this world. But we do have certain controls over our environment. For example, what we subject ourselves to, particularly in the world of entertainment, does affect our thoughts, our desires, and our behavior. When we hear and see something on a regular basis that promotes values out of harmony with God's will, we are setting ourselves up for a fall; when we play with fire, we'll eventually get painfully burned!

Much of what passes today for entertainment is flagrant enticement to commit sexual sin. Popular music also often carries the same immoral theme, as does current literature. Our society at large is characterized by a condoning attitude toward immorality. Fortunately, we can usually recognize such obvious influences and seek to shun them. But we also must be aware of and avoid the more subtle messages. One subtle message we frequently hear is that if you're really in love, sexual intercourse should happen, regardless of your marital status. Such messages are sometimes more powerful than flagrant violence and sex.

 Pray, asking God to help you answer the following question honestly in your heart.

▶ **16. What sources of temptation does Satan use in your life? Make a list and then determine what you can do to avoid those temptations. It may mean disconnecting cable television, canceling a magazine subscription, or avoiding certain places. Search your soul carefully. The changes you make may ultimately keep you from horrible consequences.**

_____

_____

_____

_____

Principle 4. Some people yield to sexual temptation not because of uncontrollable lust but because of a fear of rejection and a loss of position.

Joseph's temptation was sexual. But it was more. He had to know that he was in danger of losing everything he had gained. If he rebuffed his master's wife, she would be upset with him and could cause him a lot of grief. He would naturally fear rejection and loss of position. And as the story unfolded, that's exactly what happened. Joseph was in a no-win situation. But, as evident from Joseph's life, a single temptation may have several facets touching other areas of our lives.

▶ **17. We need to realize that immorality is not as pretty as Hollywood makes it seem. Go through the list below and write out how the following people can be hurt by immorality.**

The spouse

_____

_____

Children

_____

_____

Fellow church members

_____

_____

Unsaved people who know that the person is a Christian

_____

_____

Temptation also focuses on material things, which may be legitimate in themselves. Furthermore, a temptation for material things also can be intricately related with sexual temptation. The apostle John summarized this most clearly when he wrote,

> *"Do not love the world or anything in the world. If anyone loves the world, the love of the Father is not in him. For everything in the world—the cravings of sinful man, the lust of his eyes and the boasting of what he has and does—comes not from the Father but from the world. The world and its desires pass away, but the man who does the will of God lives forever" (1 John 2:15–17).*

Principle 5. When we resist temptation, we may pay a price with people but not with God.

Joseph did pay a painful price for resisting Potiphar's wife—imprisonment. But eventually God honored him for his righteous stand. And God will do the same for us. People may reject us, scoff at us, and even lie about us, trying to make us look bad. But God will never forget or forsake us!

We must remember also that Joseph's experience was both a temptation and a trial. This is difficult to comprehend, for God does not tempt us; Satan does (James 1:13). But God does allow trials in our lives in order to strengthen our faith (1 Pet. 1:6–7). In addition, He is often preparing us for greater responsibility in His kingdom. And, to complicate matters in our minds, God can actually take evil (which is caused by Satan) and make it work for good (Rom. 8:28).

Eventually, Joseph would see the Romans 8:28 principle work in his own life.

Small-Group Meeting 2

Opening Prayer

Begin your time together with prayer. Ask God to help you approach this lesson about Joseph and Potiphar's wife with an expectant heart, one that is looking to be challenged to live a life of sexual purity.

Building Relationships

Ask two or three people to tell about when God demonstrated His faithfulness to help them through a time of temptation. Guide the discussion carefully here, looking for non-sexual examples. As a follow-up to what is shared, ask what Scriptures were especially helpful to those group members during that time. Read 1 Corinthians 10:12–13 aloud as an example.

Reviewing the Lesson

1. The primary theme of this lesson challenges us to live a life of sexual integrity. Read aloud Genesis 39:2–12.

2. The other theme emphasized in this lesson is the faithfulness of God to Joseph. Note the things in these verses that point to God's faithfulness.

3. Joseph was faithful to God. In what ways did he demonstrate that faithfulness, and what was the result?

4. Read again Genesis 39:9. What two reasons did Joseph give when he refused to have sex with Potiphar's wife? Restate in your own words each aspect of Joseph's perspective on sexual immorality. Encourage several people to help with this question.

5. From Part 4 (beginning on page 32), what five principles are given to help us live a life of sexual integrity?

6. In what ways does this lesson demonstrate the emphasis of Lesson 1—that we should always do what is right and trust God for the outcomes?

Applying the Truths to Life

Select interactive questions to discuss as a group. Some are intended for personal reflection and are not for sharing with the group. Be careful to choose ones that are for open discussion. Include some from each of the four parts of the lesson.

Significant ones to include in this discussion are #5 and #6 (page 24), #8 (page 27), #10 (page 29), #14 (page 32), #15 (page 33), and #17 (page 34).

Ministering to One Another

Is there someone in the group who needs to rely not only on God but also on you? Read aloud Galatians 6:2. Perhaps God is at this time wanting your small group to help bear the burden of another. Ask Him to make you aware of such a need. It might be someone in your group or someone whom a member of your group knows.

Reaching Out to Others

If yours is an open group, did you set an empty chair in your circle? What will you do to fill it next time you meet?

Closing Prayer Time

Have everyone take out their prayer sheets and go through them item by item, asking for an update. The group leader can start keeping a special page of answered prayers. When the study group finishes this guide, it will be a special blessing to look over the list of prayer requests that became praises because you prayed. As the group grows more familiar with one another and develops greater trust that confidences will be kept, the requests will become more specific. Remind all of the importance of keeping confidences. These prayer times will help the group discover opportunities to minister to one another.

Close your time together with another prayer time. Pray specifically that God would impress upon each heart the absolute necessity of living a life of sexual integrity. Allow for a time of quiet prayer, encouraging each to ask Him to help them see the areas or situations in which they may be failing and to make a personal commitment to purity.

*I*ntegrity Incarcerated

Genesis 39:20–40:23

For most of us, at some point in our lives someone has done something to us that we believe was unfair and unjust. The wrongdoer may have been a family member, teacher, friend, or employer. The wrong may have happened at home, church, school, or on the job. It may have taken place many years ago when we were children, or it may have been just yesterday. It may have happened once or many times. It may have involved harsh words, rejection, a rumor, physical abuse, false accusations, or unjust criticism. Or it may have been as simple as being taken for granted or being used for selfish purposes. Furthermore, it may have been malicious or inadvertent. It some instances, it just may have been our own perception of the situation. But whatever happened, it was painful.

Joseph knew exactly what it was like to be treated unfairly and unjustly. His brothers put him in a pit and sold him as a slave. In Potiphar's house, he was falsely accused of attempted rape and thrown into prison. His only "crime" was that he was handsome and committed to living a life of integrity.

Joseph had every reason to develop a bitter spirit. The treatment he received from his brothers could have been an excuse for bitterness toward family members. The false accusation by Potiphar's wife could have been another excuse for bitterness, against women in general perhaps. Being imprisoned by Potiphar instead of being believed could have been yet another excuse. Humanly speaking, who could argue with Joseph if he had become a bitter old man? But he did not.

What can we learn from Joseph's example and how he handled injustice? For most of us, of course, his mistreatment makes anything we have experienced seem insignificant. On the other hand, any kind of injustice is emotionally painful and affects our behavior—both in the midst of the difficulties as well as when they are over. Joseph is a powerful example in both situations.

► 1. What are your "excuses" for bitterness? Consider the following settings. Are there any specific events or situations that contribute to bitterness in your heart?

Your home (present or previous)

_____

_____

Your job

_____

_____

Your church

_____

_____

In this lesson we will see how Joseph did not allow bitterness to affect either his attitude or conduct. And we will learn valuable principles on how to keep bitterness out of our lives.

PART 1: Interacting with the Scripture

Reading/Hearing God's Word

Read or Listen to:

☐ Genesis 39:20–23

☐ Genesis 40:1–23

☐ 1 Peter 2:18–21

► 2. Read or listen to the passages of Scripture listed in the margin. As you begin, ask God to speak to you through His Word. Watch for verses or ideas that are especially meaningful to you today. Once you finish, check the box indicating the passage(s) you read or listened to.

Meditating on God's Word

► 3. Now write a brief summary of a meaningful verse or idea you just noticed.

_____

_____

_____

_____

Genesis 39:20–23

"Joseph's master took him and put him in prison, the place where the king's prisoners were confined.

"But while Joseph was there in the prison, the LORD was with him; he showered him with kindness and granted him favor in the eyes of the prison warden. So the warden put Joseph in charge of all those held in the prison, and he was made responsible for all that was done there. The warden paid no attention to anything under Joseph's care, because the LORD was with Joseph and gave him success in whatever he did."

Understanding God's Word

▶ **4. Read again the focal passage for this week's lesson in the margin (Gen. 39:20–23). Underline any key words or phrases that seem especially meaningful to you.**

▶ **5. Look back at these verses. Circle one of the underlined words or phrases that you would like to understand or experience more fully.**

Looking through the Scripture to God

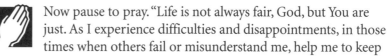 Now pause to pray. "Life is not always fair, God, but You are just. As I experience difficulties and disappointments, in those times when others fail or misunderstand me, help me to keep a right heart attitude. May I desire Your blessing on me. Keep my focus on You and my eyes off the things I experience that could bring about bitterness in my soul."

PART 2: Instead of Bitterness, Joseph Demonstrated Right Character (Gen. 39:20–23)

To resist temptation and be rewarded is one thing. To resist and get into serious trouble is another. From a human perspective, Joseph paid a terrible price for his faithful stand (39:11–20). Under ordinary circumstances, a man accused of attempted rape in the Egyptian culture would have been put to death. But how much more so when it involved the wife of Potiphar, who was "chief of the executioners"! A simple command would have meant Joseph's head—immediately.

Why did Potiphar have mercy on Joseph? Certainly, God's hand of protection was upon him, for God had a unique plan for his life. But Potiphar may have suspected his wife was lying. Perhaps his anger was directed more at her than at Joseph. After all, to save face he would now have to take action against the man who had brought him so much success. Considering his own prominent position in Egypt, he had no choice. He had to do something. He chose to allow Joseph to live—but in prison.

This prison was "the place where the king's prisoners were confined" (v. 20). It was the same prison into which the Pharaoh's chief cupbearer and chief baker would be placed. They would be put "in custody in the house of the captain of the guard, in the same prison where Joseph was confined" (40:3). Remember that "the captain of the guard" was Potiphar, which means that the prison was a room attached to Potiphar's house. Joseph's confinement was probably no more than house arrest, but it was still prison. In fact, Joseph called it "a dungeon" (40:15). If Potiphar had fully believed his wife, Joseph would not have made it to this prison. His execution would have been immediate.

Still, he experienced harsh treatment there. Psalm 105:18 says that "they bruised his feet with shackles, his neck was put in irons." Warren Wiersbe comments that this suffering put "iron" in his soul. He also notes that "young people who avoid suffering never develop real character."[1] Joseph's character was certainly tested and developed by his sufferings. He had gone from the pit where his brothers put him to the prison where Potiphar confined him.

When Joseph was a slave in Potiphar's house, God blessed him in obvious ways. Ultimately he was promoted to the position of being the chief steward of Potiphar's house. "Potiphar put him in charge of his household, and all he owned" (39:5). It was the best of what could have been a bad situation. If any bitterness had been in his heart, it would have been against his brothers. Yet there was none, as we will see in a later lesson. Had there been bitterness in his heart against them, then the pattern of responding to others with resentment would have already begun.

What Potiphar's wife then did to Joseph, with her false accusation of attempted rape and Potiphar's perhaps halfhearted acquiescence to her accusation, would have fanned the smoldering embers of bitterness into full flame. But it did not. This is evident by what happened next. The following installment in Joseph's life story sounds repetitious. And it was—by divine design! We can see five similarities between Joseph's experiences in Potiphar's house and in prison.

God's Continual Presence (vv. 2, 20–21)

First, when Joseph was scorned by his brothers and sold into Egyptian slavery, God did not forsake him. And when he was sent to prison by Potiphar, again, the Lord stayed by his side. God never forgot Joseph, nor did He leave him.

▶ **6. We also have the promise of God's presence. What does the name "Immanuel" mean? See Matthew 1:23 in the margin.**

_____

_____

Matthew's Gospel opens with the account of "Immanuel" and closes with the promise of His continued presence in 28:20. How does that verse encourage you today?

_____

_____

Matthew 1:23

"'The virgin will be with child and will give birth to a son, and they will call him Immanuel'— which means, 'God with us.'"

Matthew 28:20

"'And teaching them to obey everything I have commanded you. And surely I am with you always, to the very end of the age.'"

A Trustworthy Man (vv. 4, 21)

The second similarity is Joseph's trustworthiness. When he began his duties as Potiphar's slave, he demonstrated positive attitudes and "found favor in his eyes." Similarly, God granted Joseph "favor in the eyes of the prison warden." Both men noticed his character. He was a model slave and a model prisoner.

▶ **7. The "Protestant ethic" stresses the virtue of hard work. What do the following verses teach us about work?**

Ephesians 4:28

"He who has been stealing must steal no longer, but must work, doing something useful with his own hands, that he may have something to share with those in need."

Ephesians 4:28

_____

_____

2 Thessalonians 3:10

"For even when we were with you, we gave you this rule: 'If a man will not work, he shall not eat.'"

2 Thessalonians 3:10

_____

_____

Colossians 3:23

"Whatever you do, work at it with all your heart, as working for the Lord, not for men."

Colossians 3:23

_____

_____

1 Corinthians 4:12

"We work hard with our own hands. When we are cursed, we bless; when we are persecuted, we endure it."

1 Corinthians 4:12

_____

_____

Unusual Responsibility (vv. 4, 22)

Third, because of Joseph's faithfulness, combined with God's presence, this young man was promoted and given a high-level supervisory task, first in Potiphar's household and then in prison. In both situations he was given overall and complete responsibility.

Incredible Delegation (vv. 6, 23)

The fourth similarity demonstrates the results of trust. Both Potiphar and the warden turned everything over to Joseph and did not worry about a thing. Apparently they came to the point in their ability to trust Joseph that they did not even check up on him. They delegated everything to him and put him totally in charge. They knew he would not let them down.

▶ **8. The Bible has much to say about stewardship and our responsibility to be faithful stewards. A steward (1) is not an owner but a manager, (2) seeks the greatest possible good of his master, (3) to whom he is accountable. How did Joseph demonstrate the qualities of a good steward?**

As a manager

_____

_____

_____

In seeking what was good for his master

_____

_____

_____

In his accountability

_____

_____

_____

Consistent Success (vv. 3, 23)

The fifth and final similarity is the most important. It indicates why these men trusted Joseph so completely. Both men saw a definite correlation between the God Joseph worshiped and the success he enjoyed. Neither Potiphar nor the prison warden missed seeing this divine connection. The "God factor" was highly visible. Both men were greatly impressed.

▶ **9. In your opinion, what is success . . .**

as the world defines it?

_____

_____

_____

Job 22:21–25

"'Submit to God and be at peace with him; in this way prosperity will come to you. Accept instruction from his mouth and lay up his words in your heart. If you return to the Almighty, you will be restored: If you remove wickedness far from your tent and assign your nuggets to the dust, your god of Ophir to the rocks in the ravines, then the Almighty will be your gold, the choicest silver for you.'"

Deuteronomy 28:2

"All these blessings will come upon you and accompany you if you obey the LORD your God."

2 Chronicles 26:5

"He sought God during the days of Zechariah, who instructed him in the fear of God. As long as he sought the LORD, God gave him success."

as God defines it ?

_____

_____

_____

Match the Scripture with the principle it teaches:

___ seeking God   a. Job 22:21–25

___ obedience   b. Deuteronomy 28:2

___ submission   c. 2 Chronicles 26:5

Part 3: Instead of Bitterness, Joseph Demonstrated Right Conduct (Gen. 40:1–23)

Joseph knew firsthand what mistreatment really was. He must have thought it would never end. Though he undoubtedly struggled with bouts of anger and depression, he did not allow bitterness or self-pity to wither his soul. Joseph is a marvelous example of Christlike behavior in the Old Testament.

In His Special Responsibilities (vv. 1–4)

Joseph's attitudes and actions throughout the whole ordeal were incredibly exemplary for one who had been so mistreated by his own family and was now innocently incarcerated by the man whose trust he refused to violate. Eventually Joseph was rewarded with a degree of freedom and unusual responsibility within the prison itself. One day he was assigned two men who were not typical prisoners—the "cupbearer and the baker of the king of Egypt" (v. 1). These men held two very responsible positions.

The cupbearer was so highly trusted that he tasted the king's food and drink to make sure no one would attempt to poison him. Furthermore, the king usually took his cupbearer into his confidence, seeking his advice on very important matters.

The baker likewise was a very trusted man. He supervised all food preparation. If anyone was going to try to assassinate the king, it would probably begin in the king's kitchen. In this sense, the cupbearer and the baker worked closely together to protect their sovereign. If someone did slip poison into the king's food and drink, the cupbearer unfortunately would be the first to discover it—probably after it was too late to save his own life. He was very dependent, then, on the baker to keep it from happening in the first place.

Joseph's assignment shows that this was not the typical prison either. Potiphar had put these two men in the prison and "assigned them to Joseph, and he attended them" (v. 4). The Hebrew verb translated "attended" means "to wait on." It is the same verb used in Genesis 39:4 to describe what Joseph had done for Potiphar. He met the needs of and waited upon these new fellow prisoners. Some prison! The cupbearer and baker were essentially assigned a butler named Joseph. Because of their high-level positions in the king's court, Potiphar must have given them special privileges and treatment. When he assigned Joseph to them, he knew they would get special care.

► **10. Is your conduct dependent upon your circumstances? For example, when given an assignment at work you think is beneath you, do you:**

   a. Complete the task begrudgingly?

   b. Harbor a grudge against the one who assigned it to you?

   c. Do the minimum necessary?

   d. Do it to the glory of God?

Your response should be *d*, but the question is, "Which really describes you?"

In His Concern for Others (vv. 5–7)

When you mix heaping portions of discouragement and self-pity together, the result is complaint. To complain is a natural response, but it causes a person to look negatively on everything around him and to focus only on self. Nothing else, and especially no one else, matters.

Joseph may have had a twinge of self-pity when he said, "I was forcibly carried off from the land of the Hebrews, and even here I have done nothing to deserve being put in a dungeon" (v. 15). But that is all he said about his situation, and there is no evidence that he wallowed in self-pity.

Instead, Joseph demonstrated a special concern for those around him who were also unfortunate. Granted, in caring for the cupbearer and baker he was merely following his assignment, but he went beyond the call of duty when he saw that they were dejected and asked, "Why are your faces so sad today?" (v. 7). His character was right and it showed in his conduct. Instead of joining the ranks of his fellow prisoners in their discouragement, he showed that he was genuinely concerned and looked to help them.

► **11. Do you notice the needs of others? When is it easiest to notice others?**

☐ When at home enjoying a nice meal

☐ When driving the speed limit on the interstate

☐ While hurrying along through a crowd on a downtown street

☐ When helping with a meal at a homeless shelter

☐ Other _____

Now, when is it hardest to notice?

☐ When in the hospital for outpatient surgery

☐ When job hunting because your company is downsizing

☐ When you are passed over for a promotion

☐ Other _____

How does "self" keep us from noticing others?

_____

_____

In His Witness for God (vv. 8–23)

Both men had dreams on the same night (v. 5). The content of each dream was so uniquely related to each man's vocation and so similar in other respects that they instinctively must have known their dreams were not just a bizarre manifestation of their subconscious anxiety and fear.

They told Joseph what had happened, but made it clear that they didn't understand the meaning of these dreams. His response reflected his own growing relationship with God in the midst of difficulties as well as his boldness in telling others what he believed. "Do not interpretations belong to God?" he asked. "Tell me your dreams" (v. 8). This final statement by Joseph let them know—and anyone else who might have been listening—that he believed God would help him explain the meaning of their dreams.

► **12. Do you give glory to God? How could you draw attention to God when:**

being congratulated on a job well done?

_____

_____

sharing good news the doctor gave you?

_____

_____

enduring a time of emotional struggle?

_____

_____

viewing beautiful scenery with a friend?

_____

_____

The cupbearer spoke first. He saw a vine with three branches that very quickly produced grapes. He then saw himself squeezing the juice into Pharaoh's cup and serving him (vv. 9–11).

Interpreting the dream, Joseph told the cupbearer that in three days he would be restored to his position. But Joseph then added a personal request: "When all goes well with you, remember me and show me kindness; mention me to Pharaoh and get me out of this prison" (v. 14).

The chief baker was watching and listening intently. Perhaps he had been hesitant to share his dream for fear the interpretation may not be favorable to his future welfare. And understandably so! Though certain elements in the two dreams were similar, some were different. And the chief baker was smart enough to know that his dream might be pointing to some serious consequences.

Nevertheless, he drew courage from Joseph's positive response to the cupbearer's dream and related his own. In his dream, he was carrying three baskets of food containing "all kinds of baked goods for Pharaoh." However, as he walked along, carrying the baskets on his head, the birds swooped down and ate out of the baskets (vv. 16–17).

Joseph's response was just as quick as before and just as succinct. But his interpretation was bad news, just as the baker had feared. "The three baskets are three days," Joseph said—which was the similarity with the cupbearer's dream. Unfortunately for the baker, there was a dissimilarity. "Within three days," Joseph stated, "Pharaoh will lift off your head and hang you on a tree. And the birds will eat away your flesh" (vv. 18–19). Hearing these words, the baker must have become paralyzed with fear!

Charles Swindoll observes, "You have to respect Joseph's integrity. He knew the dream meant that the guy was going to be killed. Who wants to deliver that message? He could have told the baker anything. . . . But Joseph was a man who told the truth. He was not winning friends; he was representing God."[2]

In three days, everything happened just as Joseph said it would (vv. 20–22). Pharaoh restored his cupbearer to his previous position, but he had the chief baker executed. "The chief cupbearer, however, did not remember Joseph: he forgot him" (v. 23). Here was yet another excuse for Joseph to become bitter. But he did not, and we must not either.

PART 4: Keeping Bitterness Out of Our Lives

Paul told the church at Rome, "Do not repay anyone evil for evil. Be careful to do what is right in the eyes of everybody. If it is possible, as far as it depends on you, live at peace with everyone. . . . Do not be overcome by evil, but overcome evil with good (Rom. 12:17–18, 21). Joseph could easily have surrendered to the pull of bitterness and repaid evil for evil, but he did not. Neither can we. The following principles can keep bitterness out of our lives.

Principle 1. We must not allow bitterness to capture our souls.

Humanly speaking, Joseph had every reason to develop a bitter spirit. There had to be moments in his life when he was angry. After all, he was human. But there's a difference between getting angry and letting "the sun go down" while we're still angry. As Paul stated in his letter to the Ephesians, this is what gives "the devil a foothold" in our lives (Eph. 4:26–27). Anger that is not dealt with will lead to lingering bitterness and other kinds of sinful behavior. And in the end, we not only hurt others but also ourselves. Bitterness and an unforgiving spirit are intensely self-destructive—emotionally, physically, and spiritually.

► **13. What does Paul want us to do with bitterness according to Ephesians 4:31?**

_____

_____

_____

Ephesians 4:26–27

"'In your anger do not sin': Do not let the sun go down while you are still angry, and do not give the devil a foothold."

Ephesians 4:31

"Get rid of all bitterness, rage and anger, brawling and slander, along with every form of malice."

What warning against bitterness is given in Hebrews 12:15?

_____

_____

Hebrews 12:15

"See to it that no one misses the grace of God and that no bitter root grows up to cause trouble and defile many."

Don't misunderstand. This does not mean we cannot speak out against injustice even when that injustice is directed toward ourselves. Joseph did. He very clearly explained to the cupbearer that he had been mistreated and didn't belong in Egypt, let alone in an Egyptian prison. But he waited for God's timing, which is always a unique opportunity to defend ourselves without being or appearing defensive.

Why was Joseph able to handle this incredible and persistent mistreatment so well? That leads us to the next principle from his life.

Principle 2. We must not allow ourselves to turn against God; rather, we must turn to God even more.

Many people who are mistreated direct their bitterness not only toward those who caused it but also toward God. They blame the Lord for allowing their trouble to happen.

Think about Joseph for a moment. Though he was not perfect and certainly was naive in his relationship with his brothers, in his heart he was reaching out to help them. Furthermore, he was only doing what his father had asked him to do. And in Egypt, he resisted temptation so as not to violate God's will or Potiphar's trust in him. Yet he was terribly mistreated for doing what was right.

Do you think Joseph was ever tempted to blame God? We believe so. But he did not allow that temptation to result in sinful attitudes and actions. Rather, he grew in his relationship with God. Joseph trusted the Lord to be with him and to help him endure these crises.

In this sense, Joseph was living out the powerful truth stated by the apostle Peter, who, writing to Christian slaves in the first-century church, exhorted:

"Submit yourselves to your masters with all respect, not only to those who are good and considerate, but also to those who are harsh. For it is commendable if a man bears up under the pain of unjust suffering because he is conscious of God. But how is it to your credit if you receive a beating for doing wrong and endure it? But if you suffer for doing good and you endure it, this is commendable before God. To this you were called, because Christ suffered for you, leaving you an example, that you should follow in his steps" (1 Pet. 2:18–21).

Fortunately, most of us have not had to face this kind of mistreatment. But how do we respond to the mistreatment we do face? No

Romans 8:28, 35, 37

"And we know that in all things God works for the good of those who love him, who have been called according to his purpose. . . . Who shall separate us from the love of Christ? Shall trouble or hardship or persecution or famine or nakedness or danger or sword? . . . No, in all these things we are more than conquerors through him who loved us."

matter what the emotional or physical pain, we must not allow ourselves to become bitter toward God; for if we do, we will only compound our problem. Not that God will turn against us. He never will. His love is unconditional. The problem is that we when we turn against Him, we are violating all the necessary steps we must take to draw on Him as our divine source of strength and help.

▶ **14. Read Romans 8:28, 35, 37 in the margin. Then list all the things that Paul says are not to separate us from the love of God.**

_____

_____

_____

How could Satan use these things to make us bitter against God?

_____

_____

_____

Principle 3. In some situations, particularly those beyond our control, we must patiently wait for God to vindicate us and to honor both our faith and our positive attitudes.

This must have been the most difficult thing Joseph had to do. Of his first 11 years in Egypt, most of that time was spent in prison. Following the request he made to the cupbearer, we're told that another two years elapsed before the cupbearer remembered what Joseph had done for him (41:1).

Once again, he had to wait patiently for God to set the record straight. Joseph believed in God and trusted Him. He also continued to live a life of integrity even in prison. As we pointed out in Lesson 1, when we truly believe that God is sovereign, we will commit to living a life of integrity, trusting God for the outcomes. Joseph did that. He stayed true to God's plan, living a life of integrity every day.

Small-Group Meeting 3

Opening Prayer

Begin this meeting with a time of silent prayer. Allow everyone to go "one on one" with God for a moment, asking Him to help each commit to living a life of integrity, doing what is right no matter what the outcomes. The leader, or someone appointed by the leader, can conclude this time of silent prayer by praying aloud.

Building Relationships

We all have times when our integrity is tested. Ask if someone has a story to share about a time that he or she had a choice to make, and it was a matter of integrity. Perhaps someone knows of a situation where another person experienced difficulty as a result of doing what was right.

Reviewing the Lesson

1. Remind the group of the focus of this lesson: keeping bitterness out of our lives. Ask, "What events did you read about in this lesson that Joseph could have used as excuses for bitterness?"

2. Joseph was promoted while in prison. What two things combined to bring this about?

3. In what ways did Joseph demonstrate right conduct?

4. Have someone recount the dreams of the cupbearer and baker along with the interpretations given by Joseph.

5. At the conclusion of Part 3, one more thing is noted that could have caused bitterness. What was it? (See page 47.)

Applying the Truths to Life

Select interactive questions from this lesson to discuss as a group. Be careful to choose ones that are for open discussion, since some are intended for personal reflection and are not for sharing with the group. Include some from each of the four parts of the lesson.

Significant questions to include are #6 (page 40), #7 (page 41), #9 (page 42), #12 (page 46), and #13 (page 47).

Since the focus is on keeping bitterness out of our lives, give the group a practical step to take. Pass out index cards or small pieces of paper. Then lead the group in prayer, asking God to bring to your mind the people against whom you harbor bitter feelings. After prayer, instruct the group to write down the name(s) of the person or people brought to mind and use the card as a prayer reminder. Pray that God would remove the bitterness and show you how to have a right relationship with those on that list. This is a private exercise, not intended for group sharing.

Ministering to One Another

Ask group members to relate some of the opportunities they've had to help bear the burden of someone else. (Their examples do not have to be about how they helped someone who is part of your group.) Next, talk about specific things that members could do for others in the coming week.

Reaching Out to Others

If yours is an open group, did you set an empty chair in your circle? What will you do to fill it the next time you meet? Remember, if you do not plan for it, your group probably won't grow. In the closing prayer time, pray for people by name whom you will invite to the next group meeting.

Closing Prayer Time

Review your prayer sheets and ask for updates. Then allow members to share new prayer requests. Encourage members to be open with the group, but remind everyone of the importance of keeping confidences.

The Puzzle Pieces of Life

Genesis 40:23–41:57

The boxes that contain puzzles have two important bits of information on them. One is a picture of what the puzzle will look like when all the pieces are fitted together. It is always good to know that! Imagine trying to put together a puzzle without knowing what the picture is. The other thing the box tells you is how many pieces are in the puzzle. The more pieces there are, the more challenging the puzzle.

Most puzzle enthusiasts prefer pouring out the pieces, finding all the straight edges, and making sure the printed side is facing up. Then they start matching up pieces that look like the picture on the box, working on the easier parts first.

But imagine this scenario. What if you got only one look at the picture and did not know how many pieces were in the puzzle? To make matters worse, what if you had to put it together by pulling only one piece at a time from a bag with no picture and using the pieces in the order drawn? Each piece had to be put in place before the next one was picked. Sounds like quite a challenge!

Life, though, is often like that bag of puzzle pieces. We do not have a picture of what the puzzle will look like when completed; we do not know the number of pieces; and we cannot sort them out in advance. Instead, we reach into the bag, pull out one piece at a time, and keep fitting them together.

Joseph had a glimpse of what his life would look like. God had given him two dreams, both of which involved others bowing down to him. Then he started getting the puzzle pieces of his life, most of which did not look anything like the picture. The coat of many colors seemed to fit the picture, but what happened after that did not. He was thrown into a pit by those who were supposed to bow down to him. Instead of ascending into a position of honor, he descended into a position of dishonor, being sold as a slave. Then in Potiphar's house he advanced—only to be accused of attempted rape and thrown, this time, into prison. Anytime the picture started to improve, the next piece of the puzzle was a devastating blow. His reputation was built upon his integrity, yet it was his integrity that was attacked.

Read or Listen to:

☐ Genesis 40:23–41:40

☐ Genesis 41:41–57

Genesis 41:41–57

"So Pharaoh said to Joseph, 'I hereby put you in charge of the whole land of Egypt.' Then Pharaoh took his signet ring from his finger and put it on Joseph's finger. He dressed him in robes of fine linen and put a gold chain around his neck. He had him ride in a chariot as his second-in-command, and men shouted before him, 'Make way!' Thus he put him in charge of the whole land of Egypt.

"Then Pharaoh said to Joseph, 'I am Pharaoh, but without your word no one will lift hand or foot in all Egypt.' Pharaoh gave Joseph the name Zaphenath-Paneah and gave him Asenath daughter of Potiphera, priest of On, to be his wife. And Joseph went throughout the land of Egypt.

"Joseph was thirty years old when he entered the service of Pharaoh king of Egypt. And Joseph went out from Pharaoh's presence and traveled throughout Egypt. During the seven years of abundance the land produced plentifully.

(continued on next page)

▶ **1. Looking at Joseph's life might remind you of your own! Perhaps as you are doing this study, you are thinking about the puzzle pieces of your life. Take a moment to think about things that have happened to you that don't seem to make sense. Make a list of your puzzle pieces. You might not be able to make a picture of them now, but perhaps later you will.**

_____

_____

_____

Who would blame Joseph if he gave up? His continued trust in God's faithfulness was put to the test. Now, though, the picture of his life starts to take recognizable shape.

PART 1: Interacting with the Scripture

Reading/Hearing God's Word

▶ **2. Read or listen to the passages of Scripture listed in the margin. As you begin, ask God to speak to you through His Word. Watch for verses or ideas that are especially meaningful to you today. Once you finish, check the box indicating the passage(s) you read or listened to.**

Meditating on God's Word

▶ **3. Write a brief summary of a meaningful verse or idea you just noticed.**

_____

_____

_____

Understanding God's Word

▶ **4. Read again the focal passage for this week's lesson in the margin (Gen. 41:41–57). Underline any key words or phrases that seem especially meaningful to you.**

▶ **5. Look back at these verses. Circle one of the underlined words or phrases that you would like to understand or experience more fully.**

Joseph collected all the food produced in those seven years of abundance in Egypt and stored it in the cities. In each city he put the food grown in the fields surrounding it. Joseph stored up huge quantities of grain, like the sand of the sea; it was so much that he stopped keeping records because it was beyond measure.

"Before the years of famine came, two sons were born to Joseph by Asenath daughter of Potiphera, priest of On. Joseph named his first-born Manasseh and said, 'It is because God has made me forget all my trouble and all my father's household.' The second son he named Ephraim and said, 'It is because God has made me fruitful in the land of my suffering.'

"The seven years of abundance in Egypt came to an end, and the seven years of famine began, just as Joseph had said. There was famine in all the other lands, but in the whole land of Egypt there was food. When all Egypt began to feel the famine, the people cried to Pharaoh for food. Then Pharaoh told all the Egyptians, 'Go to Joseph and do what he tells you.'

"When the famine had spread over the whole country, Joseph opened the storehouses and sold grain to the Egyptians, for the famine was severe in all the world."

Looking through the Scripture to God

Now pause to pray. "How I thank You, God, that You are in control and know what the future holds for me. Help me to be faithful and patient, knowing that one day I will be with You forever and all the events of my life will be in the past. Help me to trust You even when life does not make sense."

PART 2: Getting The Puzzle Pieces Out (Gen. 40:23–41:40)

Joseph had a hope beyond hope. That's what kept him from despair throughout this terrible ordeal. His faith was in God—not in Potiphar, not in the cupbearer, not even in the Pharaoh. Men had failed him but he never gave up hope in God.

▶ **6. You probably know the hymn "Great Is Thy Faithfulness." Do you know where that title is found in the Bible? Read Lamentations 3:22–23 below:**

"Because of the LORD'S great love we are not consumed, for his compassions never fail. They are new every morning; great is your faithfulness."

A "lamentation" is which of the following?

a. ___ a happy poem

b. ___ a sorrowful poem

c. ___ a hopeful poem

(The correct answer is *b*.)

Now read Lamentations 3:19–21 in the margin on the next page. How is your understanding of and appreciation for the words "great is your faithfulness" affected by reading these verses?

_____

_____

_____

A Ray of Hope (40:23–41:8)

When Joseph interpreted the cupbearer's dream, reassuring him
that he would be reinstated to his former position, he asked this high-
ranking official to put in a good word for him to the king. This must
have been Joseph's first ray of hope for release since his confinement to
prison by Potiphar. Joseph certainly saw this opportunity as an answer
to his prayers.

Every day after his encounter with the cupbearer and the chief
baker, he waited for some word, for some indication that Pharaoh was
concerned about him. After all, if the cupbearer told the whole story,
Pharaoh would have known that Joseph had interpreted his dream
accurately. Surely Pharaoh would be interested in discovering more
about Joseph's ability, since it was nothing new for the king to consult
magicians and wise men who could predict the future.

But no word came. Days turned into weeks and weeks into months
and months into two full years! "The chief cupbearer, however, did not
remember Joseph; he forgot him" (40:23). What hope Joseph had must
have faded. Remember, God had not revealed to him what was going
to happen. Yet he did not allow bitterness to grip his soul, and he fulfilled his duties faithfully without complaining.

▶ **7. Our words can give others hope, but when we do not follow
through, we can disappoint them. Have you said and "forgotten"
any of the following?**

☐ "We want to have you over to our home for a meal sometime."

☐ "I'll be praying for you."

☐ "The check will be in the mail right away!"

What are some other things easily said but not done?

_____

_____

Pharaoh's Two Dreams (41:9–13)

Dreams played a very important part in Joseph's life. Many years
before, his own dreams made his brothers terribly jealous and angry
and caused them to sell him as a slave to the Midianite merchants
(37:19–20). And now, years later, it was his God-given ability to interpret dreams that would secure his release from prison and bring a promotion that would affect not only his destiny but the destiny of the
Egyptians, of his own family, and of Israel as a nation (41:1–8).

Two years after the cupbearer had been reinstated—probably again on Pharaoh's birthday—the king had a dream. He saw seven well-fed cows grazing in the Nile River. Then he saw seven undernourished cows come up out of the Nile. They immediately devoured the seven well-fed cows (vv. 1–4).

Chances are, Pharaoh wasn't too puzzled about this first dream. However, he had a second dream. This time seven healthy heads of grain were devoured by seven "thin and scorched" heads of grain (vv. 5–7).

Pharaoh immediately saw the similarities and contrasts in the two dreams. In both dreams there was a "set of sevens" followed by a second "set of sevens." The first set of sevens involved prosperity and the second set of sevens involved a lack of prosperity—an obvious contrast. Similarly, the second set of sevens in both dreams devoured the first set of sevens.

Understandably, he wanted to know what these dreams meant. "His mind was troubled, so he sent for all the magicians and wise men of Egypt" (v. 8). It must have been an impressive parade, perhaps lasting over a period of weeks, as the magicians and wise men made their appearance before the Pharaoh only to fail. No one could interpret the dream. Watching all of this was the cupbearer, who then remembered his own experience with Joseph. Or perhaps he just gained enough courage to talk about what he had forced himself to forget. Whatever his thoughts, he came to Pharaoh and said, "Today I am reminded of my shortcomings" (v. 9). It appears he actually felt guilty for not remembering Joseph's request two years before.

The cupbearer recounted the time he spent in prison as a result of Pharaoh's anger. He also told the king about this "young Hebrew" who was there. He probably had even forgotten Joseph's name, but he remembered he had been a servant of Potiphar. "We told him our dreams," the cupbearer continued, "and he interpreted them for us, giving each man the interpretation of his dream" (v. 12).

What must have impressed Pharaoh most was the fact that "things turned out exactly" as Joseph had stated they would (v. 13). He immediately sent for Joseph, who was released from the dungeon and given the opportunity to shave and change his clothes. He then appeared before Pharaoh.

Joseph's Great Opportunity (vv. 14–40)

After two long, hope-dimming years had past, Joseph unexpectedly was summoned into the presence of Pharaoh. He was not hesitant to speak about God in the presence of Pharaoh, who was himself considered a god. Rather than try to impress the king with his own abilities, Joseph said, "I cannot do it, but God will give Pharaoh the answer he desires" (v. 16). Joseph kept the focus off himself and on God.

Proverbs 2:12–22

¹² "Wisdom will save you from the ways of wicked men, from men whose words are perverse, ¹³ who leave the straight paths to walk in dark ways, ¹⁴ who delight in doing wrong and rejoice in the perverseness of evil, ¹⁵ whose paths are crooked and who are devious in their ways.

¹⁶ "It will save you also from the adulteress, from the wayward wife with her seductive words, ¹⁷ who has left the partner of her youth and ignored the covenant she made before God. ¹⁸ For her house leads down to death and her paths to the spirits of the dead. ¹⁹ None who go to her return or attain the paths of life.

²⁰ "Thus you will walk in the ways of good men and keep to the paths of the righteous. ²¹ For the upright will live in the land, and the blameless will remain in it; ²² but the wicked will be cut off from the land, and the unfaithful will be torn from it."

Just as he had done two years before, Joseph gave an instant interpretation. There were no incantations, no religious exercises, no pagan practices, as the magicians would have done. He simply and succinctly told Pharaoh the meaning of both dreams. "The dreams of Pharaoh are one and the same," Joseph reported. "God has revealed to Pharaoh what he is about to do" (v. 25).

Joseph then went on to interpret the dreams. The first sets of seven referred to seven years of great abundance, and the second sets of seven referred to seven years of famine. And to make sure Pharaoh really understood the seriousness of the prediction, Joseph told him that "the reason the dream was given . . . in two forms" was so Pharaoh would know that what was going to happen had been "firmly decided by God" and would happen soon (v. 32).

There before him, Joseph could see a plan unfolding that God had designed all along (vv. 33–36). He knew that Pharaoh was listening intently and was open to suggestions. So, he made a very wise—and brave—proposal: "And now let Pharaoh look for a discerning and wise man and put him in charge of the land of Egypt" (v. 33).

Pharaoh did not have to look far. The man was standing before him. "You shall be in charge," he replied (v. 40).

▶ **8. Do people see you as wise? Read Proverbs 2:12–22 in the margin. Note the benefits of wisdom and write them in the space provided.**

vv. 12–15

_____

vv. 16–19

_____

vv. 20–22

_____

Pharaoh recognized that Joseph was a wise man. Which of the three benefits of wisdom do you see illustrated in Joseph's life while he was in Potiphar's house?

_____

_____

PART 3: Putting the Pieces Together
(Gen. 41:41–57)

Joseph was now at the point where the events in his life, particularly the painful ones, were starting to make sense for the first time. God had been at work, even when he did not realize it. God's divine pattern for his life must have come into focus rather suddenly when he was promoted so quickly and so dramatically.

"I hereby put you in charge" (vv. 41–46)

The privileges, power, and prestige that went with this promotion accentuate why this event is so dramatic and incredible, and indeed a miracle of God.

Geographical control. Joseph was responsible for all of Egypt, a nation in ancient history comparable in influence and size only to the Babylonian Empire.

Financial authority. "Pharaoh took his signet ring . . . and put it on Joseph's finger" (v. 42). This gave Joseph an unlimited budget. With the king's ring, he could stamp any invoice, authorize any expenditure, and pay any amount to carry out the king's business.

Social prestige. Pharaoh dressed Joseph in royal garments. He provided him with a kingly wardrobe, and each garment was made of "fine linen," the most exquisite fabric in all of Egypt. Furthermore, he "put a gold chain around his neck" (v. 42).

Royal privileges. Pharaoh also provided Joseph with a private chariot—comparable to a presidential limousine in our culture today. Being second-in-command, he was assigned a group of men who rode ahead of him and cleared the way (v. 43). In addition, these men made sure people honored Joseph's presence, insisting that they "bow the knee" before him (KJV).

Political power. Joseph's greatest honor came when Pharaoh informed him that no one would make a decision regarding Egyptian affairs without Joseph's advice and approval. "I am Pharaoh," he said, "but without your word no one will lift hand or foot in all Egypt" (v. 44). Joseph became one of the most esteemed, most respected, and most powerful men in the world of his day.

▶ **9. How easy it would have been for Joseph to become a proud man! He had it all, but nothing in Scripture indicates that he lost his humility. The following verses, which you can read in the margin on the next page, give instruction to help keep us from becoming sinfully proud. Read each verse and then write out the warning it gives about pride.**

Proverbs 6:16–17

"There are six things the LORD hates, seven that are detestable to him: haughty eyes, a lying tongue, hands that shed innocent blood."

Proverbs 11:2

"When pride comes, then comes disgrace, but with humility comes wisdom."

Proverbs 13:10

"Pride only breeds quarrels, but wisdom is found in those who take advice."

Proverbs 16:18

"Pride goes before destruction, a haughty spirit before a fall."

Proverbs 29:23

"A man's pride brings him low, but a man of lowly spirit gains honor."

Proverbs 6:16–17

_____

Proverbs 11:2

_____

Proverbs 13:10

_____

Proverbs 16:18

_____

Proverbs 29:23

_____

Religious position. Pharaoh changed Joseph's name to Zaphenath-Paneah (v. 45). Inherent in the term *nath* is the idea that "God speaks and lives." Though in the minds of the Egyptian priests this referred to one of their gods, it was Pharaoh's attempt at indicating that he believed and wanted others to believe that Joseph was no ordinary man. In his own pagan way, he was trying to acknowledge Joseph's God, who had helped Joseph interpret his dreams. Remember that in Egyptian religious life, there was always room for another god.

Seven Years of Plenty (vv. 47–49)

Throughout Egypt, Joseph supervised the gigantic storehouse operation. He "stored up huge quantities of grain, like the sand of the sea," in every city. In fact, the surplus became so great that Joseph "stopped keeping records." The sheer quantity of grain "was beyond measure" (v. 49).

Seven Years of Famine (vv. 53–57)

The years of abundance came to an end, "just as Joseph had said" (v. 54). The famine that followed affected more than Egypt; it spread throughout the world. Soon, all the countries came to Egypt to buy grain from Joseph.

PART 4: The Picture Begins to Emerge (Gen. 41:50–52)

God's plan for Joseph was on schedule. His preparation was tailor-made for the task God had for him. And because Joseph passed each test, benefited from each experience, and learned to trust God more, he was ready when God opened the door of his greatest opportunity. He persevered with patience and performed his duties faithfully and successfully.

The trials of our lives will make us either bitter or better. Joseph's experiences were far more intense than anything most of us will have to endure. Think of the times he must have painfully reflected on that horrible day when his brothers stripped him of his ornamented robe and threatened to kill him. He also endured false accusations and unwarranted punishment. And to top it off, he was forgotten by a man for whom he did an enormous favor.

But in all of this, God did not forget Joseph, and Joseph did not allow bitterness to wrap its tentacles around his troubled soul. Nevertheless, he was just as human as anyone of us—and the emotional pain must have been almost more than he could bear at times.

Proverbs 4:23–27

23 "Above all else, guard your heart, for it is the wellspring of life. 24 Put away perversity from your mouth; keep corrupt talk far from your lips. 25 Let your eyes look straight ahead, fix your gaze directly before you. 26 Make level paths for your feet and take only ways that are firm. 27 Do not swerve to the right or the left; keep your foot from evil."

▶ **10. Proverbs 4:23–27 gives us specific things we should do to keep our heart right before God. Read these verses in the margin and note below the specific actions you should follow.**

v. 23

_____

_____

v. 24

_____

_____

v. 25

_____

_____

v. 26

_____

_____

_____

v. 27

_____

_____

God continued to work in Joseph's life in a way that brought about healing for his emotional hurts.

Free at Last

The first step in Joseph's emotional healing was certainly related to his release from prison. For the first time in 13 years, the events of his life began to make sense. He saw purpose in his suffering. Think how he must have felt when he was exonerated from a crime he didn't commit!

Respect and Honor

Another factor in Joseph's healing involved the way he was respected and honored in his new position. He went from being a prisoner whom everyone looked down on to being a man everyone looked up to! Pharaoh trusted him totally and gave him absolute authority. As Joseph traveled throughout the land, everyone paid respect to him. Those who went before him actually shouted, "Make way!" More literally, people were told to "bow down" before Joseph. He received the same respect and honor as Pharaoh himself.

For a man who had been sold as a slave and then incarcerated in chains and shackles, this honor must have overwhelmed Joseph. It certainly contributed to his emotional healing. This kind of position and prestige would help anyone forget humiliating pain from the past.

Seven Years of Abundance

God granted Joseph instant success in his new role. His position in Egypt was reinforced by seven years of unusual abundance (41:47–49). The land produced "huge quantities of grain"—more than ever before. His prophetic interpretation of Pharaoh's dream became a reality, and everyone would have associated these bumper crops with Joseph himself.

The "success factor," however, was not a new experience for Joseph. As we saw in Lesson 2, "the LORD gave him success in everything he did" when he first served in Potiphar's house as a servant (39:3). And when Joseph was sentenced to prison, the Lord also "gave him success in whatever he did" (39:23).

This was important in Joseph's ability to cope with the rejection he felt from his brothers and the pain he experienced from the false accusations Potiphar's wife made against him. No human being can survive without an element of success, especially when bombarded with painful experiences. But any success Joseph experienced during the first 13 years paled in comparison with the success he experienced as prime minister of Egypt. Needless to say, this helped Joseph "forget" the painful emotions associated with the past.

▶ **11. Sometimes people find it very difficult to get over things that happened to them in the past. A man like Joseph gives us hope and an example. Read the following verses in the margin and note what help God promises to us today.**

1 Corinthians 15:10

_____

_____

2 Corinthians 1:3–4

_____

_____

2 Corinthians 12:9

_____

_____

1 Corinthians 15:10

"But by the grace of God I am what I am, and his grace to me was not without effect. No, I worked harder than all of them—yet not I, but the grace of God that was with me."

2 Corinthians 1:3–4

"Praise be to the God and Father of our Lord Jesus Christ, the Father of compassion and the God of all comfort, who comforts us in all our troubles, so that we can comfort those in any trouble with the comfort we ourselves have received from God."

2 Corinthians 12:9

"But he said to me, 'My grace is sufficient for you, for my power is made perfect in weakness.' Therefore I will boast all the more gladly about my weaknesses, so that Christ's power may rest on me."

A Heritage from the Lord

After Joseph's promotion and "before the years of famine came," his wife, Asenath, gave birth to two sons (41:50). Note the names Joseph gave these two boys and what these names meant. This is a significant clue for understanding more fully how God brought healing to Joseph. This experience also illustrates what Solomon wrote centuries later: "Sons are a heritage from the LORD, children a reward from him" (Ps. 127:3).

Manasseh: "God Has Made Me Forget." Joseph named his first son "Manasseh," literally meaning "one who causes to forget." He then explained why he chose this name. "It is because God has made me forget all my trouble and all my father's household" (v. 51). The connection is clear; there is a definite cause-effect relationship between Manasseh's birth and Joseph's ability to forget his painful past.

God enabled Joseph to forget his pain and the emotional sting of his trials. He was not in bondage to past hurts. There was no lingering bitterness, no inhibiting fear, no debilitating emotional sensitivity, and no obsessive thoughts or compulsive behavior. Joseph had no regrets. God had healed his emotional memories. It is as if he were saying, "God has Manassehed me—He has removed the sting from my memory."

Ephraim: "God Has Made Me Fruitful." Asenath bore Joseph a second son. Again, Joseph chose a name that focused on what God was doing in his life (v. 52). "Ephraim" comes from a root word meaning "to be fruitful."

There are two possible interpretations regarding why Joseph named his second son Ephraim. By "fruitful," did he mean that God had given him a wife and two sons? Or was he referring to his position and accomplishments in Egypt? First and foremost, he was probably referring to his family. God had made him fruitful in giving him two sons. But God also had made him fruitful in giving him position, wealth, and success in Egypt. There's only one way to describe what was happening to Joseph both in his family life and in his political life—God had made him fruitful in the land of his suffering (v. 52).

With this statement, Joseph lets us know he had not forgotten what he had suffered in Egypt. But he also lets us know he was now rejoicing in what God had both allowed and done in his life. He understood both the trial and now his triumph. And his trial only served to make him stronger and more appreciative of God's present blessings and emotional healing in his life.

▶ **12. Most Christians are familiar with Romans 8:28. The verse begins with the word *and*, which means it is tied to what was said before it. Not only does God work for the good in all things but also . . . .**

Read the following verses in Romans 8 (in the margin) and note what else God gives to encourage and help us.

vv. 18–21

_____

_____

vv. 22-25

_____

_____

vv. 26-27

_____

_____

who searches our hearts knows the mind of the Spirit, because the Spirit intercedes for the saints in accordance with God's will."

God was at work as He had been all along. Joseph continued to do right and trust God for the outcomes. The puzzle pieces were starting to look like a picture. Nations were bowing down before him. A great abundance of grain had been gathered.

But one piece of the puzzle was still missing—his family. As Joseph was managing the affairs of the nation, God was working through the growl of hungry stomachs. Ten men were on their way, unknowingly bringing with their hunger the final piece of the puzzle.

Small-Group Meeting 4

Opening Prayer

Begin your time together with prayer. Ask God to help you approach this lesson about Joseph with an open heart. Be willing to let the Holy Spirit reassure you that God is in control even during times when life doesn't make sense.

Building Relationships

Allow group members to share a blessing God brought into their lives since the last time the group met. Ask if the blessing was unexpected. There probably were times that Joseph wondered if God would ever bless him! Then He did, and Joseph realized that God had been at work in his life all the time. Perhaps the blessings your group shares will be similar. The person may not have seen how God was working until the special blessing was evident.

Reviewing the Lesson

1. Ask someone to state in his own words the opening illustration about the puzzle pieces. Perhaps someone could tell about a time in his life when the pieces didn't make sense but later, in God's timing, they came together.

2. What puzzle pieces did Joseph have at this point? How clear do you think the picture God had planned was to him?

3. Review the puzzle pieces from Joseph's life discussed in Part 2. It is easy to simply list the basic pieces by name, so take it a step further and ask those who respond something more about those puzzle pieces: What was the ray of hope? Recount Pharaoh's dreams. Describe the great opportunity that came to Joseph.

4. When Pharaoh appointed Joseph prime minister, what were the five immediate results?

5. Fill in the blank: The trials of our lives will make us either _____ or _____. Discuss why this is true.

6. What events helped bring healing for Joseph's emotional hurts?

Applying the Truths to Life

Select interactive questions to discuss as a group. Be careful to choose ones that are for open discussion since some are intended for personal reflection and are not for sharing with the group. Include some from each of the four parts of the lesson.

Questions to consider from this lesson include #6 (page 53), #8 (page 56), #9 (page 57), #10 (page 59), #11 (page 61), and #12 (page 62).

Ministering to One Another

Perhaps things are going smoothly for you right now, but you may know of others who are having difficulties. They may feel like life is a bunch of puzzle pieces and have no clear picture of God's plan for them. Think of someone who needs encouragement and plan what you can do individually or as a group to help that person.

Reaching Out to Others

If yours is an open group, did you set an empty chair in your circle? What will you do to fill it next time you meet? If yours is a closed group, begin discussing the possibility of a couple of people from your group leading others through this same study.

Closing Prayer Time

Go through your prayer sheets item by item and ask for updates. Then share new prayer requests. Remind the group of the importance of keeping confidences, and close your time together praying for each other. These prayer times will help group members discover opportunities to minister to one another.

*H*onesty on Trial

Genesis 42–45

When you make a list of people in the Bible who modeled integrity, Joseph has to be on it. He lived a life of integrity and trusted God for the outcomes. That is the expected result when a person lives a godly life. "If God is the pattern, integrity is the result."[1]

Integrity—or a lack of it—is still an issue today. Evidence of that fact is readily available. "We have all heard of national figures whose reputation and integrity have been tarnished by scandals. From presidents to televangelists to athletes, we know examples of people whose integrity has been lost. In our communities, we can identify lesser-known people who also have succumbed to worldly desires and forfeited their integrity."[2]

Maintaining our integrity should be central to our lives. When we consider the subject of integrity, the examination must be inward because a study on integrity is a study about ourselves. Warren Wiersbe says, "[Integrity] involves all of us who profess to trust and serve Jesus Christ." He goes on to point out that "a person with integrity is not divided (that's duplicity) or merely pretending (that's hypocrisy). . . . People with integrity have nothing to hide and nothing to fear. Their lives are open books."[3]

▶ 1. How is your integrity in the following areas? Take a few minutes for self-examination, asking yourself if there is anything in these aspects of your life that you hide, hoping no one discovers it.

Work

_____

_____

Home

_____

_____

Read or Listen to:

☐ Genesis 42:1–38

☐ Genesis 44:1–13

☐ Genesis 45:1–3

Genesis 42:8–20

"Although Joseph recognized his brothers, they did not recognize him. Then he remembered his dreams about them and said to them, 'You are spies! You have come to see where our land is unprotected.'

"'No, my lord,' they answered. 'Your servants have come to buy food. We are all the sons of one man. Your servants are honest men, not spies.'

"'No!' he said to them. 'You have come to see where our land is unprotected.'

"But they replied, 'Your servants were twelve brothers, the sons of one man, who lives in the land of Canaan. The youngest is now with our father, and one is no more.'

"Joseph said to them, 'It is just as I told you: You are spies! And this is how you will be tested: As surely as Pharaoh lives, you will not leave this place unless your youngest brother comes here. Send one of your number to get your brother; the

(continued on next page)

Church

_____

_____

Every day we are confronted with issues of integrity. So was Joseph. One day a group of men stood before him and said, "Your servants are honest men." In reply he declared, "No!" and accused them of being spies (42:11–12). Those men were his ten half-brothers, the ones who sold him into slavery and lied to his father about his death. Now they were claiming to be "honest men."

Some might think that Joseph had only two choices: believe them or not. But there was a third choice. He put them to the test. The man of integrity put their honesty on trial.

PART 1: Interacting with the Scripture

Reading/Hearing God's Word

▶ **2. Read or listen to the passages of Scripture listed in the margin. As you begin, ask God to speak to you through His Word. Watch for verses or ideas that are especially meaningful to you today. Once you finish, check the box indicating the passage(s) you read or listened to.**

Meditating on God's Word

▶ **3. Write a brief summary of a meaningful verse or idea you noticed.**

_____

_____

_____

_____

Understanding God's Word

▶ **4. Read again the focal passage for this week's lesson in the margin (Gen. 42:8–20). Underline any key words or phrases that seem especially meaningful to you.**

▶ **5. Look back at these verses. Circle one of the underlined words or phrases that you would like to understand or experience more fully.**

rest of you will be kept in prison, so that your words may be tested to see if you are telling the truth. If you are not, then as surely as Pharaoh lives, you are spies!' And he put them all in custody for three days.

"On the third day, Joseph said to them, 'Do this and you will live, for I fear God: If you are honest men, let one of your brothers stay here in prison, while the rest of you go and take grain back for your starving households. But you must bring your youngest brother to me, so that your words may be verified and that you may not die.' This they proceeded to do."

Looking through the Scripture to God

 Now pause to pray. "As I study how Joseph put his brothers to the test to see if they truly were honest men, may Your Spirit search my heart, O God. May this lesson impress upon me the importance of integrity so that if there is a time that my honesty is put on trial, I will pass the test and bring glory to Your name."

PART 2: Honesty on Trial (Gen. 42)

As we pointed out in Lesson 1, two themes are evident when we study the life of Joseph: God's sovereignty and Joseph's integrity. Two of the most painful events of Joseph's life were caused by the lack of integrity of others.

▶ **6. Using any resources you have, write in your own words a definition for the two words below. (If you are studying this as a small group, discuss this question and complete it together.)**

Sovereignty is

_____

_____

Integrity is

_____

_____

The first painful event was when his brothers sold him into slavery. Perhaps Joseph heard his brothers explaining to the Midianite caravan who this slave was that they were willing to sell. The Midianites believed the ten of them over whatever protests Joseph offered. Then there was the accusation of attempted rape. Potiphar's wife, enraged by his repeated refusals to go to bed with her, lied. Joseph was removed from his position of responsibility in the house and thrown into prison.

His time in the pit and in prison was the result of the actions of unscrupulous people. Still, Joseph was very concerned about integrity and honesty, working diligently to be a trustworthy man. Now, to be able to once again trust his brothers, Joseph needed to know and believe two things—that they were telling him the whole truth, and that they were truly repentant for what they had done, both before God and man. That's why he put them to the test.

► 7. If we do something that violates trust, we should try to rebuild it with total honesty and true repentance. Keep this in mind as you study this lesson. Then look for and note below the chapters and verses in which Joseph's brothers demonstrated these.

Total honesty

_____

_____

True repentance

_____

_____

Honest! (vv. 1–13)

The "seven years of great abundance" had come and gone in Egypt and the "seven years of famine" had hit full force—in Egypt and in other countries. The land of Canaan was not exempt. Fortunately, Jacob had learned via the "nomadic internet" that there was grain in Egypt. His sons were evidently sitting around wringing their hands and "looking at each other" (v. 1). Jacob chided them for their irresponsible behavior and told them to go down to Egypt and buy food. God used this famine to bring the sons of Jacob face to face with their brother Joseph.

► 8. What evidence of God's sovereignty do you find in these verses?

Genesis 41:53

_____

_____

Genesis 42:2

_____

_____

Genesis 42:6

_____

_____

Genesis 41:53

"The seven years of abundance in Egypt came to an end."

Genesis 42:2

"He continued, 'I have heard that there is grain in Egypt. Go down there and buy some for us, so that we may live and not die.'"

Genesis 42:6

"Now Joseph was the governor of the land, the one who sold grain to all its people. So when Joseph's brothers arrived, they bowed down to him with their faces to the ground."

When they arrived in Egypt, Joseph's brothers were ushered into his presence without realizing that he was now prime minister of the land. Imagine for a moment what Joseph must have felt when he looked up and saw ten men bowing low before him. Though time had certainly taken its toll, he recognized them immediately (v. 7). Their tan, weather-beaten faces were those of shepherds and their beards set them off from the clean-shaven Egyptian men. As they bowed, the dreams from his adolescence resurfaced in Joseph's mind.

Though Joseph recognized his brothers, he sensed they did not know who he was. After all, he was only 17 when they last saw him and now he was nearly 40. His hairstyle reflected the Egyptian culture and he stood before them in royal garb. It's understandable why they didn't know who he was. Furthermore, in their minds he was probably dead, and dead men tell no tales! And if he weren't dead, they certainly did not anticipate meeting him in the home of a high-ranking Egyptian official.

What happened that day became a "master key" in unlocking Joseph's understanding regarding why God had allowed him to be sold into Egypt. Seeing God's purpose in it all must have helped dissipate any lingering anger he naturally would have felt at that moment. He had every opportunity to retaliate; his brothers had no choice in the matter. He was in control and they were at his mercy.

Joseph had several options. He could have imprisoned them in order to let them experience how it feels to be incarcerated in a strange land with no one to represent their case. He could have sent them back to Canaan without food, which would lead to a slow but certain death. He also had the authority to accuse them of being spies and then have them executed.

Joseph chose the third option, but for one purpose—he needed to know the truth. "You are spies!" he said (v. 9). He knew they weren't spies, but he didn't know whether they were telling him the truth about his father and Benjamin. Painful as it was, Joseph knew he had to threaten them in order to get at the truth.

Psalm 66:10

"For you, O God, tested us; you refined us like silver."

► **9. Integrity in others is important to a person of integrity. Joseph needed to put his brothers to the test. Read Psalm 66:10 in the margin. In what ways is the refining of silver like the testing God does of us?**

_____

_____

_____

_____

Joseph's brothers were shocked. "Your servants are honest men," they replied (v. 10). They defended themselves, answering all his questions. He heard them say that both his brother and father were still alive— but were they telling the truth? Joseph knew he needed to dig deeper into their souls.

Honest? (vv. 14–24)

Joseph kept the pressure on. "You are spies!" he said, "and this is how you will be tested" (vv. 14–15). Joseph intended to test both their words and their character. The Hebrew word for "testing" used here means to test in the sense of determining or finding out the value of something. It is used in Psalm 66:10 also. Joseph wanted to test their honesty, so he told them that they would not be allowed to leave Egypt until their youngest brother came. Then he put them in prison for three days to let his words sink in. Finally, he offered to keep one of them while the others returned home with grain.

Guilt has a way of coming to the surface. For more than 20 years, Jacob's sons had tried to hide their sin. They may have refused to talk about it for fear Jacob would find out. But they had not forgotten their heinous crime. Though they were probably relieved that only one of them would have to stay in Egypt, they were under great conviction because of what they had done to Joseph. While preparing to leave, they discussed their predicament openly with each other, probably acknowledging their sin for the first time in 20 years.

Joseph's strategy worked, which is clear from the biblical account: "They said to one another, 'Surely we are being punished because of our brother. We saw how distressed he was when he pleaded with us for his life, but we would not listen; that's why this distress has come upon us.' Reuben replied, 'Didn't I tell you not to sin against the boy? But you wouldn't listen! Now we must give an accounting for his blood'" (vv. 21–22).

His brothers didn't realize it, but Joseph understood every word they were saying (v. 23). Though he had become proficient in the Egyptian language, he never forgot his mother tongue. For the first time in his encounter with his brothers, he was beginning to get answers. They were all sorry for what they had done! And at this point, Joseph also learned that they thought he was dead, even though they had not killed him that awful day years ago. They were now acknowledging that they were still responsible for "his blood" once they had sold him as a slave to the Midianite merchants.

▶ **10. Repentance is more than feeling sorrow about what we have done. The repentance God desires always manifests itself in change—we recognize the wrong, admit (confess) it, and determine to do what is right.**

What did God use to get the brothers to talk openly about their sin (vv. 18–20)?

_____

_____

How did they interpret what was happening to them (v. 22)?

_____

_____

When his brothers' hearts began to soften, we catch a glimpse of what was deep in Joseph's heart. He could no longer bear to stand and listen to their conversation and watch their painful expressions. His emotions began to erupt, and before they could sense that his countenance was beginning to change, he left their presence and "began to weep." All the emotional pain he had experienced over the years blended with feelings of relief and probably even joy (v. 24).

Honesty Tested (vv. 25–38)

What happened next put their honesty to the test. As the brothers prepared to travel back home, Joseph arranged for their money to be placed in the mouths of the sacks containing the food they had bought. That night when they stopped to rest, one of Joseph's brothers discovered his money. The results were traumatic! When they discovered the same thing had happened to each of them, "their hearts sank and they turned to each other trembling and said, 'What is this that God has done to us?'" (v. 28).

As far as we know, this was the first time these men had acknowledged openly that God was involved in what was happening to them. At least to this point, the biblical record does not tell us that they even used His name. Though they talked about being "punished" because of what they had done to Joseph, they did not acknowledge the source of that punishment.

Joseph's brothers were sincerely frightened. How could they explain all of this to their father? Were they being forced to reveal all they had done to their brother Joseph? Would their father even allow them to take Benjamin to Egypt—especially if they told him what they really had done to Joseph?

When Joseph's brothers returned to Canaan, they shared everything that had happened in Egypt. Understandably, Jacob was devastated. "Everything is against me!" he cried (v. 36).

PART 3: The Reluctant Return (Gen. 43–44:13)

When the food ran out, Jacob casually said, "Go back and buy us a little more food" (43:2), as if Egypt were just down the road a bit. It was not that simple. Judah reminded him of the terms "the Man" had set down. Benjamin had to go with them. Now Jacob faced a tough choice. He could choose to let the family starve, or he could risk losing Benjamin. Reluctantly, he agreed to send Benjamin. His own words were the resigned sigh of a father who felt trapped. He felt utterly empty, and he knew that more grief might come his way.

Jacob instructed his sons to take some gifts to the Egyptian ruler and to take enough money to pay back what had been returned in their sacks of grain as well as enough to pay for a new supply. As the brothers headed off with Benjamin and the money, they were carrying the proof of their honesty. They knew that Benjamin's presence was a test, but not that the money was too.

When they arrived in Egypt, to their surprise they were taken to Joseph's private mansion (43:15–25). Predictably, they were gripped with fear, thinking they were going to be charged with stealing the silver they had found in their sacks.

They wasted no time seeking out Joseph's steward and hurriedly explained what had happened. This was a wiser move on their part than they realized! By doing this they demonstrated honesty—the very aspect of their lives that was in question.

▶ **11. Joseph repeatedly questioned whether or not his brothers were honest men. He had good reason not to trust them. Trust, a precious commodity, takes time to develop, and we must do all we can to maintain it. Evaluate your life with these questions:**

Am I doing anything in my life that might lead to a violation of trust?

_____

_____

Are there any instances in which I have violated someone's trust?

_____

_____

If so, have I made an effort to rebuild trust with total honesty and true repentance?

_____

_____

If someone has violated my trust, what am I doing to help this person rebuild that trust?

_____

_____

When Joseph arrived home, it was the moment he had been waiting for. Hardly able to contain his emotions, he surveyed the scene before him. His brothers had already said that his father was still living. Now his concern was for Benjamin. His eyes fell on the youngest—a 23-year-old. There was no way he could have recognized Benjamin. The last time Joseph had seen him, Benjamin was only a toddler.

Meeting Benjamin was too much for Joseph. He could not maintain his emotional control, so he quickly "hurried out" and "went into his private room and wept there" (v. 30).

Joseph finally regained control of himself. When he was certain they couldn't see the redness in his eyes he returned, and to his brothers' astonishment he had his servants seat his brothers chronologically—"from the firstborn to the youngest." How did he know their ages? Imagine the look in their eyes when Joseph had Benjamin served "five times as much as anyone else's" (vv. 33–34).

Think how intently Joseph must have studied their faces and their body language while Benjamin was being treated so royally. He also must have strained his ears to pick up what his brothers were saying while all of this was happening. We're not told what he saw or heard, but he must have been pleased.

Yet Joseph was still not satisfied that he had the answer to his final question. How could he be sure they had really changed? He could not judge their hearts. So he felt he must take one more step.

PART 4: One Final Test (Gen. 44:14–45:3)

When his brothers were ready to leave for Canaan, Joseph instructed his steward to give them as much food as they could carry and once again return their money. But this time he also ordered his personal silver cup to be placed in Benjamin's sack. After they were well on their way, Joseph then sent his steward after them to accuse them of stealing (44:1–14).

Predictably, Joseph's brothers were aghast! They were so certain of their innocence that they offered the life of the one who had done such a thing (v. 9). They quickly opened their sacks to prove they were not guilty. But to their astonishment, there was Joseph's silver cup in Benjamin's sack! They were so frustrated and distraught that they literally "tore their clothes" (v. 13).

Joseph had thought through this strategy carefully. He instructed his chief steward to tell his brothers before he conducted his investigation that whoever had the cup would become a slave and the rest would go free (v. 10). If they were jealous of Benjamin because he was treated so royally at the banquet, they might have been able to mask their feelings then. But they could not hide their true feelings now.

There was no question in Joseph's mind what they would have done years ago. More specifically, if Judah had responded as he did when they decided to sell Joseph into Egyptian slavery, he would have taken the lead in seeing that Benjamin bear the blame and become the slave. Furthermore, he would have done so without any consideration for the effect it would have on Jacob. But their reactions this time were different—much different. All of them, together, returned to Egypt to face this criminal charge!

Imagine Joseph's relief and joy when he saw them with their little parade of donkeys entering the palace gates. They were a pathetic sight, with heads bowed low, their garments torn, and their long, flowing hair and full beards matted by dust and tears. But to Joseph, they were now men who were more concerned about their aged father and their younger brother than they were about themselves. They had passed the test! They had changed from the inside out!

The Finishing Touch

Judah passed the test even more nobly than the others (44:15–34). When they were ushered into Joseph's house, he stepped forward. He made no excuses, uttered no rationalizations, and made no attempts to cover up their sinful actions that spanned the 22-year period. "What can we say?" he said. "How can we prove our innocence?" And he then uttered his most repentant statement to date—"God has uncovered your servants' guilt" (v. 16).

With this confession, Judah acknowledged their sin against Joseph. Though he did not mention Joseph's name, it's easy to read between the lines. But more important to Joseph was Judah's statement, "We are now my lord's slaves—we ourselves and the one who was found to have the cup" (v. 16).

► **12. Knowing we have sinned should bring sorrow to our hearts, but repentance is more than a feeling. Ultimately, true repentance brings change. It is not just an outward show of sorrow but a true change that starts on the inside. Read again Judah's speech (vv. 16-34) and answer the following:**

What did Judah say that shows he admitted that he and his brothers were guilty of sin (v. 16)?

_____

_____

_____

What did Judah say that shows he had changed (v. 16)?

_____

_____

_____

Who convicted Judah of his sin (v. 16)?

_____

_____

_____

Judah made it clear they would not forsake Benjamin. If he became a slave, they would all become slaves. Though innocent of the charge of stealing, Judah admitted that they were guilty of a much greater sin—a sin God had uncovered.

The fact Judah acknowledged that God had uncovered their sin is significant. Since they believed Joseph was dead, they were acknowledging God's sovereign intervention. Unknown to them, of course, Joseph was involved as an instrument for righteousness in the hand of God. Furthermore, the fact that they did not feel pressured into this confession by Joseph verifies the wisdom their brother exemplified in choosing to remain anonymous.

► **13. God works in our hearts not just to cause us sorrow for our wrongs but to lead us to repentance. Read 2 Corinthians 7:10 in the margin. How does the speech of Judah illustrate this truth?**

_____

_____

_____

As Joseph listened to Judah's confession, he must have yearned to enfold Judah in his arms and weep with joy. Yet he restrained himself. He had one more unanswered question in his mind. How did Judah—and his older brothers—actually feel about Jacob at this moment? What concern did they have for their aged father? Consequently, Joseph responded to Judah's confession by telling him that "only the man who was found to have the cup" would become his slave. "The rest of you, go back to your father in peace," he said (v. 17).

Judah's response must have overwhelmed Joseph, for he focused his thoughts and feelings on Jacob. He reviewed their father's response when they had returned from Egypt to Canaan the first time: "If the boy is not with us when I go back to your servant my father and if my father, whose life is closely bound up with the boy's life, sees that the boy isn't there, he will die. Your servants will bring the gray head of our father down to the grave in sorrow" (vv. 30–31).

After demonstrating great concern for their father, Judah then took the final step in his confession. He pleaded with Joseph to set Benjamin and his other brothers free and let him take his little brother's place as a slave. "How can I go back to my father if the boy is not with me?" he asked. He then answered his own question, "No! Do not let me see the misery that would come upon my father" (v. 34).

Joseph now had the answer to his final question—and more! Here stood the man who had convinced his brothers to sell Joseph as a slave to a band of Midianites now offering to be a slave in Benjamin's place. Here stood the man who years ago couldn't have cared less about the impact Joseph's death would have on his father. But now he was so concerned about Jacob that he was willing to remain in Egypt so Benjamin could return. This was true repentance!

▶ **14. Sometimes people think that they cannot change, but the Christian can stop doing what is wrong and start doing what is right. In addition, sometimes people think their sins are so far in the past that they do not need to repent. Read Romans 6:11–14 in the margin and find the following truths:**

The Christian is dead to what?

_____

What must not "reign" in the Christian's life?

_____

The Christian is to be an instrument of what?

_____

Romans 6:11–14

"In the same way, count yourselves dead to sin but alive to God in Christ Jesus. Therefore do not let sin reign in your mortal body so that you obey its evil desires. Do not offer the parts of your body to sin, as instruments of wickedness, but rather offer yourselves to God, as those who have been brought from death to life; and offer the parts of your body to him as instruments of righteousness. For sin shall not be your master, because you are not under law, but under grace."

Now go through those verses a second time and think about your own life.

What is it that God wants you to consider yourself dead to? Be specific.

_____

_____

Does God want that specific thing "to reign" in your life?

_____

_____

Instead of letting that sin "reign," God wants you to do what?

_____

_____

The Shock of a Lifetime

Hearing Judah's final statement, Joseph could contain himself no longer (45:1–3). He ordered everyone to leave the room except his brothers. Then he revealed his true identity, weeping and wailing so loudly he could be heard even beyond the confines of his mansion. Judah's confession had unraveled his soul.

Joseph's brothers were totally caught off guard. They had no clue whatsoever that the man who tested them so severely was their own brother. They were so shocked and terrified that they could not utter a word and, initially, could not accept it as reality. But what happened that day in that room is in itself another story—to be continued in the next lesson.

Small-Group Meeting 5

Opening Prayer

As you begin your time together, pray with special emphasis on the need for each one in your group to be a person of integrity. Ask God to help you approach this lesson on Joseph with a heart open to examination. Pray that your focus in this meeting will help you see the ways in which your integrity needs to be strengthened.

Building Relationships

Allow time for every member to share one thing for which they praise God.

Reviewing the Lesson

1. Ask the group to share why they think Joseph put his brothers through so much.

2. Review the series of meetings between Joseph and his brothers as well as the "tests" of putting the money and the silver cup in their sacks.

3. Note which brothers are mentioned by name in this lesson. What part did these men play in selling Joseph into slavery?

4. Contrast Judah's action when he sold Joseph with how he spoke (unknowingly) to Joseph as prime minister.

Applying the Truths to Life

Select interactive questions to discuss as a group. Be careful to choose ones that are for open discussion, since some are intended for personal reflection and are not for sharing with the group. Include some from each of the four parts of the lesson.

Questions to consider from this lesson include #6 (page 67), #8 (page 68), #10 (page 71), #12 and #13 (page 75), and #14 (page 76).

Ministering to One Another

Review activities that the group as a whole or individuals have done to encourage one another. This study has only one more lesson. Challenge the group not to stop helping others when the study is done.

Reaching Out to Others

If yours is an open group, did you set an empty chair in your circle? The final lesson is a very important one. It is not too late to invite someone. Perhaps a new attendee, along with some others from this group, would begin a new study together. Ask members of the group to consider leading another study.

Closing Prayer Time

Looking at your prayer sheets, ask for an update on each item. Then allow members time to mention new prayer requests. Remind everyone of the importance of keeping confidences, and pray as a group for the needs that are mentioned.

*H*ope-Filled Bones

Genesis 45-50

The words of a familiar hymn provided the opening line of the e-mail sent to a group of praying friends: "I am not skilled to understand what God hath willed, what God hath planned; I only know at His right hand is One who is my Saviour!"[1] A veteran missionary who had served the Lord for many years both in South America and in the home office of her mission was writing to give an update on her medical condition. The sentiments of this hymn carried special weight. How often we sing such words, but how seldom does their significance sink into our hearts. For the writer of the e-mail, however, those words best expressed her heart. She continued, "What I have to tell you has been sifted through God's sovereign will and plan."

This woman's story is a long one that progresses from the initial diagnosis of both cardiac and respiratory disease, to varied treatments, declining health, and a multitude of decisions, including the one she now shared in the note. After consulting yet another specialist, her doctors had decided to remove her from the heart/lung transplant list, having judged her as too high a risk for the procedure; and if she survived the surgery, they expected her to be on dialysis the rest of her life. The doctor who had been asked to make the final determination said that he could not make her suffer that way. His compassion would not let him proceed with something that had such a poor possibility of working.

This, now, was her response to the doctor's decision:

> "I agree. God is sovereign. I am not interested in asking 'why' God did it this way. I am disappointed, yes, that there is nothing medicine can do, but God had a reason . . . maybe to teach others lessons in faith, as well as myself. God is great, He is kind, and He certainly does not make any mistakes."

In the e-mail written shortly before she died, my (Tony's) friend expressed one of the realities of life and a faith that was strong. Her note revealed a clear spiritual perspective on the sovereignty of God.

► 1. At times the only word in our prayers is *why.* Do you recall occasions when you had to trust God, not knowing the answer to that prayer? Think about these areas of your life and note situations when you asked "Why?"

Physical health

_____

_____

Job

_____

_____

Family life

_____

_____

Death of a loved one

_____

_____

Plans that fell through

_____

_____

As we come to the concluding lesson on the life of Joseph, it is obvious that he, too, had a clear spiritual perspective on why he had to suffer. We are not told at what point Joseph came to realize so succinctly that God was in control. Perhaps it was when he saw his brothers bowing before him and he remembered the dreams of his youth. What the Bible does make plain, however, is that Joseph knew God had been working through all the events of his life.

PART 1: Interacting with the Scripture

Reading/Hearing God's Word

► 2. Read or listen to the passages of Scripture listed in the margin. As you begin, ask God to speak to you through His Word. Watch for verses or ideas that are especially meaningful to you. Once you finish, check the box indicating the passage(s) you read or listened to.

Read or Listen to:

☐ Genesis 45:1–24

☐ Genesis 50:15–21

☐ Genesis 50:22–26

Genesis 50:15–21

"When Joseph's brothers saw that their father was dead, they said, 'What if Joseph holds a grudge against us and pays us back for all the wrongs we did to him?' So they sent word to Joseph, saying, 'Your father left these instructions before he died: "This is what you are to say to Joseph: I ask you to forgive your brothers the sins and the wrongs they committed in treating you so badly." Now please forgive the sins of the servants of the God of your father.' When their message came to him, Joseph wept.

"His brothers then came and threw themselves down before him. 'We are your slaves,' they said.

"But Joseph said to them, 'Don't be afraid. Am I in the place of God? You intended to harm me, but God intended it for good to accomplish what is now being done, the saving of many lives. So then, don't be afraid. I will provide for you and your children.' And he reassured them and spoke kindly to them."

Meditating on God's Word

▶ **3. Write a brief summary of a meaningful verse or idea you just noticed.**

_____

_____

_____

Understanding God's Word

▶ **4. Read again the focal passage for this week's lesson in the margin (Gen. 50:15-21). Underline any key words or phrases that seem especially meaningful to you.**

▶ **5. Look back at these verses. Circle one of the underlined words or phrases that you would like to understand or experience more fully.**

Looking through the Scripture to God

 Now pause to pray. "God, now that I have studied these scenes from the life of Joseph, I am reminded again that You are the Sovereign of the universe. Just as Joseph did, help me to acknowledge that You know what is best for me. In times of difficulty and confusion, help me trust You and Your plan for my life. May I stay faithful to You and Your Word, living with a heart filled with hope."

PART 2: A Tearful Reunion (Gen. 45:1–24)

When Judah reached the final step in his repentant confession, actually pleading that he be allowed to take Benjamin's place as a slave, Joseph "could no longer control himself" (v. 1). The powerful urge to reveal his identity—which had almost taken over on several previous occasions—now overwhelmed him. He knew this was the time to tell them who he was. His brothers had answered all his questions. They had told the truth. He had seen Benjamin and now knew that his father was still alive as well.

More important, the hearts of his brothers had changed. They did not—and would not—treat Benjamin like they treated him more than 20 years earlier. Neither would they lie to Jacob. Rather, they were deeply concerned about his physical and emotional well-being. And most of all, Joseph's brothers had acknowledged their sin against God, followed by a deep and sincere repentance.

"Have Everyone Leave My Presence!"

All this time Joseph revealed very little emotion to his brothers. They had observed him only as a stern, rational, and cold-hearted Egyptian ruler. At times when he could not mask his feelings, he had left the room to weep in private. You can imagine what his brothers must have thought when they saw their accuser begin to lose emotional control and heard him cry out, "Have everyone leave my presence!" (v. 1).

Joseph wept and wailed "so loudly" that the Egyptian attendants he had ordered to leave the room could still hear what was happening (v. 2). We're not told how long Joseph wept uncontrollably, but one thing is certain: the ordeal lasted long enough for word to get back to Pharaoh's household.

"I am Joseph!"

When Joseph finally regained control of his emotions, he identified himself. "I am Joseph!" (v. 3).

Joseph's next question takes us even deeper into his heart. "Is my father still living?" he asked. Though he believed Judah's report, his question now was more rhetorical—revealing how much he had missed Jacob. He had believed intellectually, but he was having difficulty believing emotionally. It was as if the news of his father were too good to be true!

When Joseph's brothers heard him identify himself by name, they were so stunned and overwhelmed with fear they couldn't utter a word. We read that "they were terrified at his presence" (v. 3). They couldn't believe what they were hearing and seeing.

"Come Close to Me"

Joseph's brothers were probably leaning away from him. We tend to do that when we are not sure about something. Perhaps Benjamin was straining for a closer look at the brother he remembered in name only, but not the others. If this were Joseph, they reasoned, could revenge be far away?

"Come close to me," Joseph said. The Hebrew verb in verse 4 that is translated "close" (nah-gash) speaks of an intimate closeness and is even used occasionally for coming near to a person to embrace or kiss him. Joseph wanted his brothers not only to recognize him but also to embrace him as their brother. When they did step closer, he said, "I am your brother Joseph, the one you sold into Egypt!" (v. 4). Now they could look in his eyes and carefully search the features of his face, trying to find the 17-year-old they had sold as a slave. They looked not only for recognition but also to see his reaction to them. Was he planning revenge? Was there anger in his eyes? Did he look like one about to take out the pain of his past on those who had caused it?

► **6. How do you respond to someone who desires to be close to you? In particular, how do you overcome the distance that is the result of how they may have mistreated you?**

☐ No matter what they say, I keep my distance.

☐ I pretend that all is forgotten, but in my heart it is not.

☐ With great caution I take a step closer but keep up my guard.

☐ I work at rebuilding trust.

Whatever transpired in that intimate moment, Joseph's brothers now believed they were face to face with the one they had sold into Egypt many years before. Predictably, their fear and anxiety suddenly turned to distress and self-hatred. Shame must have consumed them. How could they look into their brother's eyes? How could they have been so evil? Their feelings of remorse, regret, and guilt must have overwhelmed them!

► **7. When your actions have caused another person to keep his distance, how do you rebuild the relationship? Make a list of things that would need to be done, such as being totally honest, repenting before God and man, and asking for forgiveness. What else might you add?**

_____

_____

_____

How important is total honesty in repairing and restoring a relationship?

_____

_____

_____

Joseph's true character shines at this moment. He quickly attempted to put them at ease, to dissipate their intense feelings of guilt. He wanted them to know that he had not tested them to make them suffer but to discover the truth, and he didn't want them to suffer now. "Do not be distressed," he pleaded. "Do not be angry with yourselves for selling me here" (v. 5).

"God Sent Me Here"

Joseph's next statement must have overwhelmed them even more—not with fear but with a sense of awe: "It was to save lives that God sent me ahead of you. . . . God sent me ahead of you to preserve for you a remnant on earth and to save your lives by a great deliverance'" (vv. 5, 7).

His next words were magnanimous, extremely sensitive, and designed to help his brothers overcome the shame they were feeling. "So then," he reassured them, "it was not you who sent me here, but God'" (v. 8). They had suffered enough. He did not want them to continue to blame themselves. Though they had committed a horrible sin, Joseph wanted them to see that God had an ultimate purpose in allowing all of this to happen (vv. 8–15).

▶ **8. It is one thing to "talk the talk" and another to "walk the walk." We can say that we accept the sovereign workings of God in our lives without really doing so. Joseph did the "talk" and the "walk." First, note what he said that pointed to accepting God's work in his life.**

_____

_____

_____

Then, using this scene and others that you have studied so far, note what he did that shows he truly accepted God's work.

_____

_____

_____

PART 3: Seeing Purpose in Suffering (Gen. 45:25–50:26)

All human beings struggle with the issue of "why bad things happen to good people." Ultimately, only God knows the answer to this question. But in the meantime, we can be sure that "in all things God works for the good of those who love him" (Rom. 8:28). We may not understand everything that happens, but we can learn a valuable lesson from Joseph, who trusted God for years even though he did not understand the purpose in his own suffering. Eventually he understood, and so will we—if not on earth, then in eternity.

"Jacob Was Stunned"

When Joseph's brothers returned from Egypt and told their aged father that Joseph was still alive, "he did not believe them." In fact, he "was stunned" (45:26). After all of those years of thinking that Joseph had been torn to pieces by a wild animal, Jacob could not respond with hope. The memory of his son's blood-stained robe must have flashed through his mind—as it had a thousand times over the last 22 years.

However, the more Jacob's sons talked and related what Joseph had said, "and when he saw the carts Joseph had sent to carry him back," his spirit revived (v. 27). It *had* to be true. There was too much evidence. Jacob must have sensed a new sincerity in his sons. They were different men. Furthermore, where would they have acquired so many things—their new clothing and the 20 donkeys "loaded with grain and bread" (v. 23)?

"I'm convinced!" Jacob cried out. "My son Joseph is still alive. I will go and see him before I die" (v. 28).

As soon as Jacob and his sons could get everything organized, they left for Egypt. On the way, they stopped in Beersheba, where Jacob offered sacrifices to God (46:1). There the Lord spoke directly to Jacob and affirmed what his sons had reported. He also assured Jacob of His personal presence as he traveled to Egypt (vv. 2–4).

Proverbs 30:7–9

"'Two things I ask of you, O LORD; do not refuse me before I die: Keep falsehood and lies far from me; give me neither poverty nor riches, but give me only my daily bread. Otherwise, I may have too much and disown you and say, "Who is the LORD?"'"

▶ **9. Never forget God when being blessed! Read Proverbs 30:7–9 in the margin, and answer the following questions.**

What did Agur (the author of Proverbs 30) pray would be kept from him?

_____

The danger of poverty is the temptation to do what?

_____

The danger of riches is the temptation to do what?

_____

How does Jacob's action in Genesis 46:1 relate to this prayer?

_____

How do you guard your heart lest you forget God?

Imagine Jacob's elation when God told him that "Joseph's own hand" would close his eyes when he died (v. 4). Though Jacob had accepted the fact that Joseph was still alive, the Lord's affirmation was proof positive that he would see his beloved son again!

A Grand Reunion

Joseph had been eagerly waiting for his dad's arrival. And what a reunion it was! He traveled to Goshen and met his father there. When he saw Jacob, he "threw his arms around his father and wept for a long time" (v. 29).

When Jacob finally gained enough emotional control to speak coherently, he uttered, "Now I am ready to die, since I have seen for myself that you are still alive" (v. 30). Try to imagine the scene. There they stood, arm in arm, weeping and rejoicing at the same time.

When Jacob died, we once again see Joseph's deep love for his father. He "threw himself upon" him "and wept over him and kissed him" (50:1). He grieved over his father's passing, but he rejoiced that he had been able to spend not only his first 17 years with his father but the last 17 years of his father's life with him as well (47:28).

After Jacob died, however, fear began to well up in the brothers' hearts. A nagging question kept going through their minds: "What if Joseph holds a grudge against us and pays us back for all the wrongs we did to him?" (50:15).

Joseph responded to his brothers' fear both with a human and divine perspective. On the one hand, he was sensitive to their fears and anxieties. He knew they were human and identified with their anguish. "Don't be afraid," he reassured them (v. 19).

Joseph was reiterating what he had said the day he had revealed his identity 17 years earlier. At that time, he told them not to "be distressed" or "be angry at themselves" (45:5). Once again, "he reassured them and spoke kindly to them" (50:21). He could not and would not retaliate.

Colossians 3:12–13

¹²"Therefore, as God's chosen people, holy and dearly loved, clothe yourselves with compassion, kindness, humility, gentleness and patience. ¹³Bear with each other and forgive whatever grievances you may have against one another. Forgive as the Lord forgave you."

▶ **10. Read Colossians 3:12–13 in the margin. Before giving the command to forgive others, Paul writes about the heart attitude we are to have. List the attitudes found in verse 12.**

How do those attitudes help us forgive others?

_____

_____

_____

Which of these attitudes do you need to work on the most?

_____

_____

"Am I in the Place of God?"

Joseph quickly explained why he would never retaliate. He was not that kind of man. He did not harbor bitterness. But even more significant than his gentle spirit and compassionate heart was the fact that his theology affected his attitudes and actions. Joseph understood God's perspective regarding what had happened. He made this divine point of view very clear when he asked his brothers a revealing rhetorical question: "Am I in the place of God?" (v. 19).

In All Things

Joseph came to see God's hand in all that had happened to him. Though there were times in Egypt when he had to trust God in the midst of total darkness and confusion, he now understood why he was sold into slavery.

Joseph had stated that reason to his brothers the day he revealed his identity (45:5–8). But he knew he must reiterate it once again with even greater emphasis—and added insight and wisdom. Seventeen years before, he made no reference to the evil part they played in it all. Instead, his focus then was on God's sovereign plan for his life as well as theirs. "It was to save lives that God sent me ahead of you," he had said (v. 5). Elaborating, he continued, "God sent me ahead of you to preserve for you a remnant on earth and to save your lives by a great deliverance. So then, it was not you who sent me here, but God" (vv. 7–8).

▶ **11. Read again Romans 8:28 in the margin and answer the following questions.**

What were some of the "all things" of Joseph's life?

_____

Romans 8:28

"And we know that in all things God works for the good of those who love him, who have been called according to his purpose."

What was the "for good" of Joseph's life?

_____

How is Romans 8:28 an encouragement for us today?

_____

What are the "all things" of your life?

_____

What assurance do you have that God will work ultimately for "good"?

_____

Joseph's brothers sinned terribly when they sold him into Egypt as a slave. They also had sinned when they lied to their father and put him through such terrible suffering. At this moment, Joseph sensed that his divine perspective on what happened was not enough to deal with their sin. His brothers needed to hear him acknowledge that what they had done was indeed wrong. And so he did! He informed them that he knew that they had "intended to harm" him. But he also blended this human perspective with his Heavenly Father's perspective. Thus he told them that even though they had sinned against him, "God intended it for good" (50:20). Though neither Joseph nor his brothers could ever fully understand this kind of paradoxical thinking, this expanded explanation put the finishing touch on their restored relationships. As far as we know, these men not only accepted God's forgiveness but also forgave themselves.

Joseph kept this divine perspective on what had happened to him until the day he died. Though he was considerably younger than most of his brothers, God took him home before they passed off the scene. Knowing he was about to depart this life, he called his brothers together one day and said, "I am about to die. But God will surely come to your aid and take you up out of this land to the land he promised . . . to Abraham, Isaac and Jacob." Then Joseph "made the sons of Israel swear an oath and said, 'God will surely come to your aid, and then you must carry my bones up from this place'" (vv. 24–25).

Joseph believed God. He knew a day would come that God would return His people to the land promised to Abraham, Isaac, and Jacob. His father was already buried there! He was so confident of God's promise and so filled with hope that he gave instructions for his burial in the Promised Land. What a strange sight it must have been years later when the children of Israel left Egypt for the Promised Land.

1 Thessalonians 4:16

"For the Lord himself will come down from heaven, with a loud command, with the voice of the archangel and with the trumpet call of God, and the dead in Christ will rise first."

1 Corinthians 10:13

"No temptation has seized you except what is common to man. And God is faithful; he will not let you be tempted beyond what you can bear. But when you are tempted, he will also provide a way out so that you can stand up under it."

James 1:5–6

"If any of you lacks wisdom, he should ask God, who gives generously to all without finding fault, and it will be given to him. But when he asks, he must believe and not doubt, because he who doubts is like a wave of the sea, blown and tossed by the wind."

There they were, trekking though the wilderness, carrying what was probably an elaborate Egyptian mummy case. That coffin carried the hope-filled bones of Joseph (Ex. 13:19).

▶ **12. Even though he did not live to see the day, Joseph believed that God would return the people of Israel to the land He promised them. Likewise, we are to be people of a confident hope, believing and knowing that God will do what He has promised. What promise do you find in the following verses?**

1 Thessalonians 4:16

_____

_____

1 Corinthians 10:13

_____

_____

James 1:5–6

_____

_____

Add some of your favorite promises of God:

_____

_____

_____

PART 4: Principles to Live By

Joseph was 110 years old when he died. As they embalmed him and placed him in a coffin in Egypt (50:26), they laid to rest an Old Testament hero. Joseph exemplified in a marvelous way what it means to be a man of character—a man who lived for God with all his heart in the good times as well as the bad. He is indeed a great model—and an example to every Christian. From him we learn principles that help us see purpose in suffering.

Principle 1. When God accomplishes divine purposes in spite of our sins, we must never excuse ourselves for doing what was wrong.

God is sovereign in all aspects of life. This was Joseph's perspective. Consequently, some people could read the story of his life and be tempted to blame God for their sin, finding in God's sovereignty an excuse for doing wrong. After all, even though Joseph's brothers had committed a horrible crime, God used it to achieve His divine purposes. So they reason, "Doesn't this put the responsibility for their actions back on God?"

James warned against this kind of thinking when he wrote, "When tempted, no one should say, 'God is tempting me.' For God cannot be tempted by evil, nor does he tempt anyone; but each one is tempted when, by his own evil desire, he is dragged away and enticed. Then, after desire has conceived, it gives birth to sin; and sin, when it is full-grown, gives birth to death" (James 1:13–15).

Jacob's sons were responsible for their sins against Joseph and their father. God did not cause these men to sin, but He used the results of their sin to accomplish His purposes. Only God can understand this antinomy. No human logic can explain it. But it's true nevertheless!

Principle 2. *While on this earth, it's not possible to explain all human suffering.*

Not all human problems and pain can be explained with Joseph's experience. God had a special plan for Joseph in allowing his suffering, and we are fortunate enough to know the end of the story. In God's scheme of things, he allowed Joseph to be able to see a specific purpose in what happened to him.

There are times, however, that Christians suffer and we may never be able to explain why. For example, how do we explain rape to a person who has been marred for life? How do we explain child abuse that leaves an individual an emotional cripple? How do we explain mental torture that drives a person insane? How do we rationalize the ravages of war that leave thousands of people dead and thousands more maimed?

Suffering in general is related to the fact that the world is contaminated by sin. There are two dimensions to this problem. First, we can use our freedom to sin and make innocent people suffer. Second, we can use our freedom to sin and cause severe suffering in our own lives. More often than not, both dimensions are interrelated.

Principle 3. *Though suffering can be difficult to explain and the reason for it may not be clear, a Christian has the potential to see meaning that others may not see.*

God can accomplish specific purposes in and through our lives when we suffer, such as the following:

We may have opportunities to communicate the Gospel of Jesus Christ. When Paul was in prison in Rome, he wrote to the Philippians and told them that what was happening to him really served to "advance the gospel" (Phil. 1:12). This also has been true in the lives of many Christians who have suffered persecution over the years. They have turned it into an opportunity to witness for Jesus Christ.

Personal suffering can help us understand the sufferings of others. Paul clearly illustrated this purpose in his second letter to the Corinthians: "Praise be to the God and Father of our Lord Jesus Christ, the Father of compassion and the God of all comfort, who comforts us in all our troubles, so that we can comfort those in any trouble with the comfort we ourselves have received from God" (2 Cor. 1:3–4).

Suffering can produce Christian maturity. James wrote that Christians should "consider it pure joy" when they "face trials of many kinds." He then states the reason: "because you know that the testing of your faith develops perseverance. Perseverance must finish its work so that you may be mature and complete, not lacking anything" (James 1:2–4).

We must not define James' use of the word *joy* as "happiness" or "pleasure." Rather, it means a deep, settled peace in the midst of pain that enables us to endure this kind of affliction, knowing we're in God's permissive will.

Suffering can bring an individual to a salvation experience. Suffering has been the occasion for some individuals inviting Jesus Christ to be their Savior. Without coming to a place of helplessness, they may never have turned to God for help. In this sense, it's better to suffer in this life than spend all of eternity separated from God!

What we believe about God and His involvement in our lives should make a difference in how we face difficult circumstances. We're all human beings, just like Joseph. And even though God had a very unusual and special purpose for allowing suffering in his life, we, too, can apply the truth in Romans 8:28 to our lives: "And we know that in all things God works for the good of those who love him, who have been called according to his purpose."

Like Joseph, we must obey God and lead lives of integrity, trusting Him for the outcomes.

Small-Group Meeting 6

Opening Prayer

Begin your meeting with prayer. Specifically thank God that He is sovereign over all things. Ask Him to help you live out that truth, trusting Him in every circumstance. Perhaps God will use this lesson to strengthen some in your group who are going through difficulties. It may be that this will be heart preparation for some yet unseen trial that will come into your life.

Building Relationships

Allow time for each member to share one thing for which they praise God.

Reviewing the Lesson

1. Read aloud the opening story about Tony's friend and her e-mail describing the doctor's decision. In what ways does her note demonstrate hope that rests in the sovereignty of God?

2. Part 2 tells about what happened when Joseph revealed his identity to his brothers. Have someone from the group briefly summarize that scene.

3. What aspects of Part 3 are evidence that God can have a purpose in our suffering?

4. Read aloud the principles to live by found in Part 4 and ask if each principle is clear to the members of the group. It would be good to do this again at the end of the study, because each principle is very important.

Applying the Truths to Life

Select interactive questions to discuss as a group. Be careful to choose ones that are for open discussion, since some are intended for personal reflection and are not for sharing with the group. Include some from each of the four parts of the lesson.

Questions to consider from this lesson include #1 (page 80), #8 (page 84), #9 (page 85), #10 (page 86), #11 (page 87), and #12 (page 89).

Now go back over the concluding principles.

Ask someone to trace through Joseph's life the twin themes of God's sovereignty and Joseph's integrity.

Conclude the study time by praying to commit to living a life of integrity, trusting God for the outcomes.

Ministering to One Another

One of the ways we can minister to others is to help each live a godly, pure life. Talk about the need to be accountable to one another. Encourage each member to develop an accountability partner.

Reaching Out to Others

Now would be a good time to talk about multiplying by dividing. Perhaps some from your group would take this study material and lead another group through it. Take what you have learned from this experience and share it with others.

Closing Prayer Time

Share prayer requests that have been answered while the group has met and prayed. Spend time praying that God will help each in the group to have a repentant heart. Pray also that each member of the group, by God's grace, will be a person of integrity.

Notes

Lesson 1

[1] Briscoe, D. Stuart. *The Communicator's Commentary Series, Old Testament, Vol. 1* (Waco, Tex.: Word Books, 1987), p. 305.

Lesson 2

[1] Hamilton, Victor P. *The Book of Genesis: Chapters 18–50* (Grand Rapids, Mich.: Wm. B. Eerdmans Publishing Co., 1995), p. 460.

[2] Bonhoeffer, Dietrich. *Temptation* (New York: Macmillan Publishing Co., Collier Books, 1953), pp. 116-117.

[3] Meyer, F. B. *Joseph: Beloved—Hated—Exalted* (Fort Washington, Pa.: Christian Literature Crusade, n.d.), p. 30.

Lesson 3

[1] Wiersbe, Warren. *Expository Outlines on the Old Testament* (Covington, Ky.: Calvary Book Room, 1968), p. 42.

[2] Swindoll, Charles. *Joseph: A Man of Integrity and Forgiveness* (Nashville, Tenn.: Word Publishing, 1998), p. 47.

Lesson 5

[1] Snodgrass, Klyne. *The NIV Application Commentary: Ephesians* (Grand Rapids, Mich.: 1996), p. 261.

[2] Hindle, James E. Jr. "The Five C's of Integrity," *Contact Quarterly, Vol. 53, No. 3*, Fall 1994, p. 9.

[3] Wiersbe, Warren. *The Integrity Crisis* (Nashville, Tenn.: Thomas Nelson Publishers, 1988), p. 21.

Lesson 6

[1] Greenwell, Dora. "I Am Not Skilled to Understand."

Interacting with God
Small–Group Covenant

Believing that God wants His people to be a healthy Body of Christ with Jesus Christ Himself as its Head, we submit ourselves to Him and to one another so that we may help one another grow into mature believers and so that, as a group, we "may be built up until we all reach unity in the faith and in the knowledge of the Son of God and become mature, attaining to the whole measure of the fullness of Christ" (Eph. 4:12-13). Together we agree to:

1. Study God's Word each week and complete the learning activities for the week's lesson prior to the group meeting.

2. Pray regularly and specifically for one another, our church, our spiritual leaders, and those who need to come into a saving relationship with Jesus Christ.

3. Attend all group meetings unless unavoidable circumstances prevent attendance. If we are unable to attend, we will make every effort to notify our group leader and let him know how the group can pray for us in our absence.

4. Participate in the meetings by listening carefully and sharing openly.

5. Keep confidential any personal matters discussed by other members during the meetings.

6. Seek to demonstrate love as the Holy Spirit leads us to help meet one another's needs.

7. Seek to bring glory and honor to God through our relationships with one another.

Signatures: **Date:** _____

_____   _____

_____   _____

_____   _____

_____   _____

_____   _____

_____   _____

_____   _____

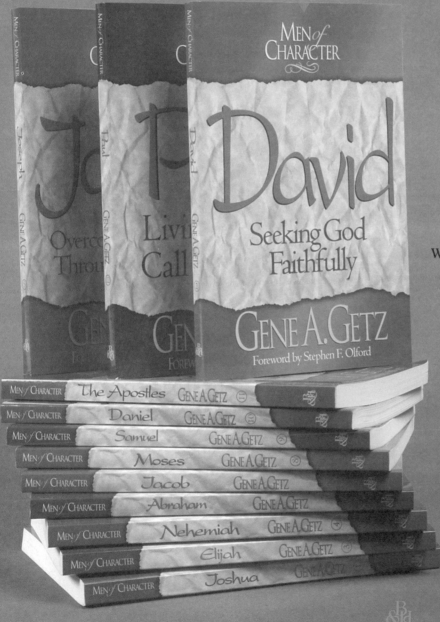